About the authors

Barbara Meardon is Diocesan Adviser for Work with Children and Families and a prima............ She has an MA in RE in the Primary School and has lectured on Religious Education on PGCE courses. She has written *Children's Quiet Days* and *Let the Children Come* (a set of reflective stations based on the United Nations Children's Charter) and edited a book of children's prayers with colleagues in Salisbury Diocese. She is also actively involved in children's ministry at Bath Abbey.

Verity Holloway trained as a primary school teacher, specialising in Religious Education. She has taught in London and Wiltshire and currently works as RE and Collective Worship Adviser for Salisbury Diocese. She has also co-written *Festival Matters* (Salisbury Diocese Board of Education, 2005) and *Love and Sex Matters* (Salisbury Diocese Board of Education, 2010, 2012) (a series of four books for Key Stages 1–4), as well as *Values for Life* (2007), *Pause for Reflection* (2004) and *Pause to Reflect on Values* (2006), published by Jumping Fish Ltd®.

Praise for *8 Bible-themed Journey Days for Primary Schools*

In religious terms, life's journey can be a pilgrimage. The biblical stories of journeys range from the epic to the intensely personal; they inform our faith and shape our character, individually and together.

An excellent resource that supports good teaching is very welcome, especially when it makes links across the curriculum in such a way that RE finds its place in the life of a healthy school. I love the way the material in this book has been tried and tested. The lessons are shared. It is of the highest quality. You will enjoy using it, so have fun.

THE RIGHT REVEREND NICHOLAS HOLTAM, BISHOP OF SALISBURY

Text copyright © Barbara Meardon and Verity Holloway 2014
Cover photos: cross, candles, dove, waterlily, stars © iStockphoto/Thinkstock; footprint © Purestock/Thinkstock; wheat © Fuse/Thinkstock; background © Hemera/Thinkstock; Celtic stonework used under licence from Shutterstock, Inc.

The authors assert the moral right
to be identified as the authors of this work

Published by
The Bible Reading Fellowship
15 The Chambers, Vineyard
Abingdon OX14 3FE
United Kingdom
Tel: +44 (0)1865 319700
Email: enquiries@brf.org.uk
Website: www.brf.org.uk
BRF is a Registered Charity

ISBN 978 0 85746 247 3

First published 2014
10 9 8 7 6 5 4 3 2 1 0
All rights reserved

Acknowledgments
Scripture quotations taken from the Contemporary English Version of the Bible published by HarperCollins Publishers, copyright © 1991, 1992, 1995 American Bible Society.
Scripture quotations taken from the Holy Bible, New International Version, copyright © 1973, 1978, 1984 by International Bible Society, are used by permission of Hodder & Stoughton Publishers, a member of the Hachette Livre Group UK. All rights reserved. 'NIV' is a registered trademark of International Bible Society. UK trademark number 1448790.
Scriptures quoted from the Good News Bible published by The Bible Societies/HarperCollins Publishers Ltd, UK © American Bible Society 1966, 1971, 1976, 1992, used with permission.
'In the beginning' by Paul Bunday, from *Spirit Borne* (BRF, 1996). Used with permission.
Blessing by Revd Dr Sandra Millar, from *Festivals Together* (SPCK, 2012). Used with kind permission of Sandra Millar.
'Wind and fire' by Carolyn Warvel, used with kind permission of Carolyn Warvel. Visit www.daniellesplace.com.

A catalogue record for this book is available from the British Library

Printed by Gutenberg Press, Tarxien, Malta.

8 Bible-themed Journey Days

for Primary Schools

A cross-curricular resource for teaching about Christianity

Barbara Meardon & Verity Holloway

Acknowledgments

We would like to thank our colleagues at Salisbury Diocesan Board of Education who have supported us through the development of the resource, and also the staff, children and volunteers from the case study schools, Combe Bissett CE VA Primary School and Christ Church CE VC Primary School in Bradford on Avon and supporting parishes.

Important Information

Photocopying permission

The right to photocopy material in *8 Bible-themed Journey Days for Primary Schools* is granted for the pages that contain the photocopying clause: 'Reproduced with permission from *8 Bible-themed Journey Days for Primary Schools* by Barbara Meardon and Verity Holloway (Barnabas in Schools, 2014) www.barnabasinschools.org.uk', so long as reproduction is for use in a teaching situation by the original purchaser. The right to photocopy material is not granted for anyone other than the original purchaser without written permission from BRF.

The Copyright Licensing Agency (CLA)

If you are resident in the UK and you have a photocopying licence with the Copyright Licensing Agency (CLA) please check the terms of your licence. If your photocopying request falls within the terms of your licence, you may proceed without seeking further permission. If your request exceeds the terms of your CLA licence, please contact the CLA directly with your request. Copyright Licensing Agency, Saffron House, 6–10 Kirby Street, London EC1N 8TS. Telephone 020 7400 3100; fax 020 7400 3101; email cla@cla.co.uk; web www.cla.co.uk. The CLA will provide photocopying authorisation and royalty fee information on behalf of BRF.

BRF is a Registered Charity (No. 233280)

Contents

Foreword 6

Introduction 7

Case studies 12

Journey days

Unit 1: Stepping out on the journey 15
       Unit 1 extension material 21
       Unit 1 church-based activity day 22

Unit 2: Creation: a perfect relationship 23
       Unit 2 extension material 31
       Unit 2 church-based activity day 33

Unit 3: Abraham and Sarah's journey 35
       Unit 3 extension material 43
       Unit 3 church-based activity day 45

Unit 4: Ruth's journey 46
       Unit 4 extension material 52
       Unit 4 church-based activity day 53

Unit 5: Jump into a picture: Christmas 54
       Unit 5 extension material 58
       Unit 5 church-based activity day 59

Unit 6: Jump into a picture: Easter 60
       Unit 6 extension material 69
       Unit 6 church-based activity day 70

Unit 7: Jump into a picture: Pentecost 72
       Unit 7 extension material 76
       Unit 7 church-based activity day 77

Unit 8: Following in Jesus' footsteps 78
       Unit 8 extension material 89
       Unit 8 church-based activity day 90

Downloadable appendices

Guidance sheet for volunteers 92

Information sheets 93

Web links 94

Foreword

This practical resource is written to introduce children to the exciting concept of journeys in the Bible, and in so doing aims to enhance the relationship between school and local church.

It contains material for an introductory day, 'Stepping out on the journey', followed by seven further workshop days. It is written by two published authors, both trained as primary school teachers and practising as RE specialists, whose voice is one of respect for children, awareness of best classroom practice, and lived faith.

From a child's perspective, going on a themed journey will allow them to travel with Abraham and Sarah or with Ruth in the Old Testament, or it might take them with Jesus as he grows up in the New Testament. The journey will allow them to ask the questions, 'What is God like?' or 'What is God's kingdom like?'

From a teacher's perspective, it is a dream come true, in that the material does not seek to replace curricular content but to complement and enhance it. It offers the expected learning goals and transferable learning skills with detailed notes for teachers at Key Stages 1 and 2. Each journey comes with notes for worship, group time and individual time, and the overall package offers different routes through it.

From a local church volunteer's perspective, the book gives clear information and guidance sheets as to what is expected, including an invaluable array of wider web links.

It is a timely and actionable resource that tempts the practitioner to get on with it immediately.

Howard Worsley
Chair of Salisbury Diocese Children and Young People Education Ministry Committee and former Diocesan Director of Education in London and the Midlands

Introduction

And as He spoke He no longer looked to them like a lion; but the things that began to happen after that were so great and beautiful that I cannot write them. And for us this is the end of all the stories, and we can most truly say that they all lived happily ever after. But for them it was only the beginning of the real story. All their life in this world and all their adventures in Narnia had only been the cover and the title page: now at last they were beginning Chapter One of the Great Story which no one on earth has read: which goes on for ever: in which every chapter is better than the one before.

C.S. LEWIS, *THE LAST BATTLE* (1956)

General guidelines

This resource has been written to introduce children to the concept of journeys in the Bible and to enhance the relationship between school and local church. Through participation in these journey days, children can explore key Christian concepts, questions and themes, including 'God is revealed' (What is God like?), 'God as companion on the journey' (How do Christians respond to God as creator, loving father and friend?) and 'Welcomed into God's family' (What is the kingdom of God like? What is the Christian community like?).

These workshop days are valuable for both schools and churches because:

- They build links between the school and the local church, enabling them to work together and build good community relationships.
- They provide an opportunity for children to encounter and explore Bible stories and Christianity in a contemporary context.
- They provide opportunities for spiritual development for everyone involved, aiming to increase reflective skills and articulacy in spiritual language.
- They provide opportunities for learning outside the classroom.
- They support RE-led integrated learning and enhance teaching and learning in RE, enabling children to learn about and from religion. This can act as a model for learning in the church context.
- They use the most up-to-date, tried-and-tested approaches to learning, including reflective storytelling, thinking and questioning techniques and multiple intelligences.

Through a creative cross-curricular programme, children will:

- learn about the concept of life as a journey.
- be offered opportunities for spiritual, moral, social and cultural development.
- experience creative, deep and immersive learning and have the opportunity to develop essentials for learning and life, including key skills, thinking and reasoning and reflection.

Ideally, the themed workshop days will be part of a joint programme for church and school together. For each journey day, material is included to extend the themes that are introduced in school and develop them in the church context through after-school clubs and special events. This is not, however, essential.

Purpose of the scheme

This scheme has been written to support teachers in the delivery of a cross-curricular theme with RE as the focus subject. It does not replace systematic study of key concepts. It does not offer a full RE curriculum or replace the study of key concepts in RE. Rather, it offers something that complements and enhances discrete subject teaching. Each unit builds on good practice in RE throughout the year, but is not intended to be the sole means of delivery. However, the findings from the pilot studies at the end of this section show that these learning events can help safeguard RE's position in an overcrowded and results-driven curriculum.

The experience and impact of the journey day is not designed to be limited to the day itself. Opportunities are included for themes and questions to be explored or revisited in both school and church contexts, with adults and children, through church-based activity days, class collective worship and 'Looking back on the journey' sessions.

Impact on learning

Integrated learning is a specific kind of learning with a synthesis of content, knowledge, skills and understandings from a variety of disciplines that enables students to see and make cross-curricular connections using various methods.

This scheme of work supports various learning goals, such as:

- transferable learning skills.
- thinking and reasoning.
- providing a student-relevant curriculum.
- exploring the same question from different angles.
- making connections throughout the curriculum and with real-life experiences.

It aims to stimulate, strengthen and enhance children's intellectual and social development as well as competence in basic skills. The integrated approach engenders community ethos within the classroom and school while children experience and/or learn a wide range of skills, dispositions and feelings.

Please note that although learning intentions are provided at the beginning of each workshop on the school days, these are for planning purposes only and should not be displayed in the lesson. This will ensure that children's responses and questions are neither pre-empted nor guided.

Using the material

This resource contains material for an introductory day, 'Stepping out on the journey', followed by seven further workshop days. The journey days can be delivered using a variety of models.

- Model 1: One unit per academic year, starting with Unit One, then choosing six units from the seven available.
- Model 2: A three-year cycle, offering one unit in autumn, spring and summer of each year. In the second and third years, Unit One would be repeated for new children in the school in the autumn term, and one of the other units would not be covered.

Multiple activity workshops are possible and could offer children a choice of response to the story.

Children can remain in class groups or be vertically/family grouped.

Preparation

In order to plan and deliver a journey day effectively, it is essential that you have a key leader or small team of people to coordinate and lead the meetings. The key person can only fulfil their role if they have no responsibility for a workshop or if they do the same workshop in rotation. The key person or group of people will require time and commitment to prepare for and lead the day.

Meetings will need to be held for school staff and for volunteers from the local church to explain the purpose and process of the scheme of work.

- Plan which journey days to do, when and how often to do them, and who will be involved.
- Plan dates and times for preparation and reflection sessions with staff, governors or PCC as appropriate, as these contribute to the process and can be overlooked in the busyness of getting ready, or forgotten afterwards.

From the pilot studies it was clear that volunteers needed to hear what the teachers wanted from the day or from an activity and to realise the value of talking and exchanging ideas.

- Suggest things the volunteers can do—how they can contribute to a session.
- Identify where people can talk from a point of view of faith.
- Appreciate that church representatives might have a different level of confidence in speaking to the class.
- Allocate church representatives to specific tasks and give clear guidelines (see suggested ideas for a guidance sheet for volunteers on page 92).
- School and church policies on CRB checks should be followed.

A balance needs to be struck between too many meetings and too few, with examples and reasoning added to the pack to ensure that all volunteers and teachers feel as comfortable as possible before and on the day.

Communication is key: keep everyone informed.

Planning the day

Decide who will set up the worship space, who will lead collective worship and how you will seat the children.

Whole-school collective worship launches the day and brings it together with a celebration at the end of the day. There is also a time for reflection in the middle of the day, which is class-based (either after afternoon registration or on the following day). This pattern of collective worship and reflection has a significant impact on spiritual development, as a user comments:

The pattern for worship and reflection made a powerfully positive contribution to the day and provided much of the sense of community as well as the 'performance of understanding'.

'My journey' reflection journal

Every child has a journal in which to record thoughts and ideas during a reflection time in the middle of each journey day or on the following school day. (The pilot days indicated that it was more successful to do the reflection on the following day.) The child adds to this book for each journey day throughout their time at the school.

A symbol to illustrate the journey is cut out and stuck on to the timeline in the 'My Journey' book. Children then generate an open or interesting question about the story and write it in their journal, or draw a picture or write about the key moment of the story and why it matters. Scribes can be used if necessary; it is important that a copy of the child's thoughts is included in the book in order for them to look back on their journey as they progress through the school. The label and timeline are downloadable from www.barnabasinschools.org.uk/9780857462473.

Workshop themes

Workshops within each of the days are organised under three themes as follows:

- Be knowledgeable
- Be communicative
- Be creative

It is important to aim for a balance of workshops, so that they are not all art- or literacy-based. This balance can be achieved in one journey day or over a series of days. Practically based workshops leave 'space' for spiritual discussion to take place.

Label for 'My Journey' reflection book

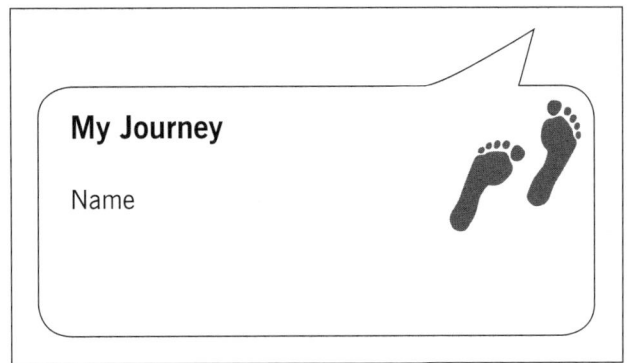

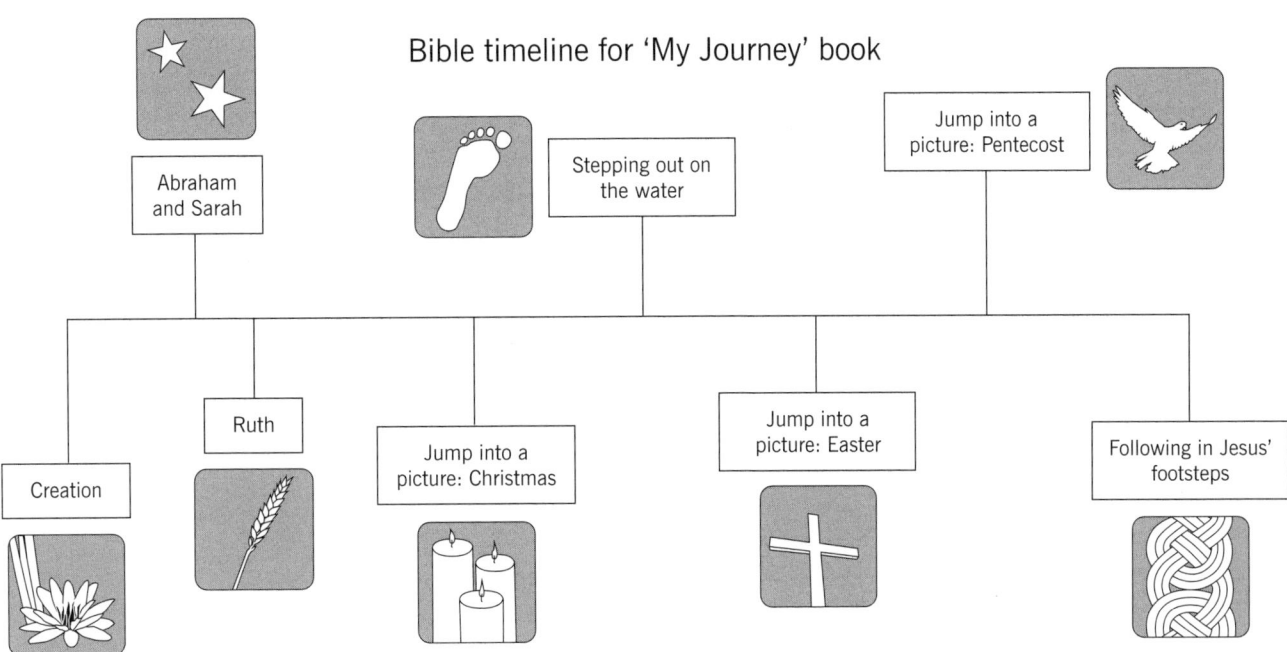

Bible timeline for 'My Journey' book

Reproduced with permission from *8 Bible-themed Journey Days for Primary Schools* by Barbara Meardon and Verity Holloway (Barnabas in Schools, 2014) www.barnabasinschools.org.uk

Specific teaching tools

PMI

PMI (Plus, Minus, Interesting) is a thinking tool that enables pupils to sort their ideas, in order to be better able to reach a decision about a question. It is important to teach this method first, using the following example, before you use it for an RE question.

- Pose the question: Would you want a third arm?
- In small groups, talk about and write down all the *advantages* (plus points) of having a third arm. Allow exactly five minutes. Explain that the children are not allowed to talk about any disadvantages at this point.
- Share ideas as a class.
- Talk about and write down all the *disadvantages* (minus points) of having a third arm. Allow exactly five minutes. Explain that the children are not allowed to talk about any advantages at this point.
- Share ideas as a class.
- Talk about the *interesting* ideas about having a third arm that are neither advantages nor disadvantages. Allow exactly five minutes.
- Share ideas as a class.
- Look at your ideas and decide on your answer to the question.

You can use this method to discuss or address RE questions posed in various workshops. Although it is used here for RE, it is an excellent tool for any subject.

Conscience alley

This is another decision-making tool. Two lines of children are formed, facing each other. One side is asked to shout out views and opinions that support a decision; the other line shouts the opposite views and opinions. A child then walks down between the two lines, listening to both sets of ideas. At the end of the lines, the child has to make a decision about which viewpoint they agree with.

Diamond sorting

This is a tool that enables children to rank ideas from most important to least important, and to discuss and justify their choices. Explain to the children that they will be expected to discuss where the ideas go in the diamond, to justify why they go there and to be able to discuss changes in the ranking together.

Write, on separate cards, the ideas that the children will rank in some way. The most important idea goes at the top of the diamond, then the next two most important, then the next three, then the next two, and the least important at the bottom. If you decided that you did not want one of the ideas to be the single least important, you could choose to sort in a triangle shape.

Once each group has sorted, you could invite the children to walk round the class and look at everyone else's answers, then discuss as a class the similarities and differences in their decisions.

Note: you can create more cards than there are spaces in the diamond shape so that the children can decide if something does not belong in the ranking.

Freeze frame

Freeze frame is used to identify key points in a story. Ask the children to act out a section of a story and freeze when they get to the most important or turning point. You could ask them to show three key points.

Hot-seating

This is an empathetic way of exploring someone else's actions and/or viewpoint. A child sits on the hot seat at the front of the class as a character from the story you are exploring. The rest of the class can ask them questions and they answer as if they are that character. The teacher can support them in their role.

Reflective storytelling

Examples of reflective storytelling would be the *Godly Play* volumes by Jerome Berryman and *Bible Storybags* and *More Bible Storybags* by Margaret Cooling. This is a method of storytelling based on Montessori principles, using physical objects and figures to tell the story in an engaging way. It includes reflective wondering questions that enable children to connect with their own feelings and the deeper meaning of the story. This type of wondering question is used throughout the units, not just in the stories. It enables the children to take risks with their thinking and ensures that you do not limit pupils' responses to short answers or the answers that they think you want.

Useful resources

The following books are those that are most often suggested for use.

Bibles (4–7 years)

- *The Big Bible Storybook*, Maggie Barfield (SU, 2007)

Bibles (7–11 years)

- *The Children's Bible in 365 Stories*, Mary Batchelor (Lion, 2001)

Bibles (whole school)

- *The Lion Storyteller Bible*, Bob Hartman (Lion Hudson, 2013)
- *The Barnabas Schools Bible*, Rhona Davies (Barnabas in Schools, 2012)

Bible information and storytelling aids

- *Godly Play Volumes 1–7*, Jerome Berryman
- *Bible Storybags*, Margaret Cooling (Barnabas for Children, 2008)
- *More Bible Storybags*, Margaret Cooling (Barnabas for Children, 2012)
- *The Big Story*, Martyn Payne (Barnabas for Children, 2011)
- *Reflect-a-Story* (TTS)
- *The Big Bible Storybook Timeline* (SU, 2009)
- *The Lion Encyclopedia of the Bible* (Lion Hudson, 2009)
- *Journey through Bible Lands*, Tim Dowley (Candle Books, 2008)
- *Life in Bible Times*, Tim Dowley (Candle Books, 2010)

Prayer and reflection aids

- *The Lion Book of 1000 Prayers for Children* (Lion Hudson, 2010)
- *Goodnight Prayers*, Sophie Piper (Lion Hudson, 2008).
- *A-cross the World*, Martyn Payne and Betty Pedley (Barnabas, 2004), downloadable from www.barnabasinschools.org.uk/9780857460998Z
- *Blob Spirituality*, Pip Wilson, available as a download (see web links, page 94)
- *Pause for Reflection* pack, available from Gloucester Diocese (Jumping Fish) (see web links, page 94).

Online Bible search engines

- www.Biblegateway.com: select New International Version – UK or New Century Version
- http://Bible.oremus.org: select New Revised Standard Version (Anglicised edition)

Music

It is desirable that your selection from the choice of suggested music reflects the wide range of styles offered. Within this resource we have included music from across the world and from different historical periods that can be used in both school and church, and we hope that you will develop a shared repertoire of hymns and songs that will enrich worship in both communities. Purchasing individual tracks in mp3 format saves money.

Suggested songs can be found in *Complete Anglican Hymns Old & New* (Kevin Mayhew, 2008 edition) unless otherwise indicated. For songs from Fischy Music, visit www.fischy.com.

Web links

You will find a complete list of URLs for all web links mentioned in this book on pages 94–96. These pages are also available to download at www.barnabasinschools.org.uk/9780857462473.

Prayer and reflection

Like the music choices, a range of prayer and reflective activities is offered from across the world, from different periods of history and in different styles. They are designed to offer opportunities for personal spiritual development to both children and adults, encouraging increased spiritual vocabulary and understanding. The structure of the programme ensures that children and adults learn from one another in this intergenerational way of working and through the shared journey in both school and church communities.

Case studies

The following case studies show how two church schools chose to run a journey day, and describe the impact of the choices they made.

School One

- Whole school (consisting of three mixed-age group classes).
- Children were in vertical groups containing children from each class.
- Due to concerns about younger children moving round the school safely, each group had an identifying badge using a symbol/colour and word linked to the theme of the day—for example, mistletoe/green or holly/red for the Christmas journey.
- Church volunteers were allocated to each group and stayed with that group as they rotated through the workshops.
- Each team of teachers and LSAs offered one of three workshops, which they chose and developed. One workshop was RE/numeracy/art/discussion-based; one was RE/art based; the third was RE/literacy based.
- Church volunteers contributed to collective worship.
- Older children supported younger children—for example, by scribing ideas.
- A number of meetings with church volunteers and staff were held both before and after the day.
- A coordinator was chosen.

Impact of vertical/family grouping

Teachers felt that vertical grouping was a major factor in the success of the day as a learning event and contributed directly to the 'Christian ethos' of the day. It was valuable to have the different age groups working together, supporting and listening, valuing and helping each other. It resulted in the older children realising that the younger ones had 'something of value to contribute' and the younger children being really proud of working with the older children.

This was corroborated by the reaction of the pupils themselves to vertical grouping: 'I know it was, for the pupils, a huge element of the day—they loved it.' It was 'really valuable for the Foundation children; it made them feel part of the whole school so much more quickly; doing it early on in the year was powerful.' Foundation children were 'so well supported by the other children'.

The challenge of vertical grouping was greater in some workshops than others—for example, in the literacy-based one: 'It was a challenge to reach all of the children but also get a learning outcome that was successful and could be celebrated by all of them and accessed by all of them.' The teacher addressed this by putting older children with younger children to be scribes and using a system of recording ideas that the older children were already familiar with in RE—having differently shaped thought bubbles for what a character might have said, thought or felt at a point in the story.

School Two (three pilot days)

- Key Stage 1 only (six classes). Children stayed in their classes.
- Pilot day 1 was class-based; pilot day 2 was in vertical/family groups with Year 6 mentors; pilot day 3 was class-based with Year 4 mentors.
- Each year group selected the workshops they wanted to do.
- Church volunteers supported in class.
- All year groups did an RE/literacy/discussion (story) workshop, an RE/art workshop and an RE/literacy (drama or poetry) workshop.
- Church volunteers contributed to collective worship.
- A number of meetings with church volunteers and staff were held both before and after the day.
- A coordinator was chosen.

Impact of being class-based

Children were comfortable in familiar surroundings, and teachers knew pupils' needs. They were able to have age-specific activities and differentiate within them. For example, Foundation had play-based and self-directed learning choices, whereas Year 2 wrote poems in response to the story. Although it gave the opportunity for shared planning and teaching within each year group, each teacher had more different workshops to plan and deliver.

Impact of Key Stage 2 (Year 4 and 6) assistants

The Key Stage 2 children prepared the day before by listening to the story and having a thinking and questioning discussion in order to establish their own ideas about it and possible meanings for themselves and others, including Christians. The Key Stage 1 children loved having the older children there. It was very interesting to see the relationships between the children develop over the day and watch the older children grow into their mentoring roles.

Findings from pilot studies

Children could see that RE is relevant to other subjects and the wider curriculum, not just a discrete subject. Teachers felt that the pupils were engaged as RE thinkers; they experienced a broadened and extended curriculum but also gained knowledge and understanding in RE and RE skills.

All teachers felt that input from the church had added to pupils' experience. The church volunteers were good models of Christian faith and knowledge; they listened and talked to the children, facilitated questioning and brought empathy to activities and learning. Teachers wrote that church volunteers brought great subject knowledge, were experts, and significantly improved the adult–child ratio. All felt that the event contributed to the ethos and aims of the school and to community cohesion, building on existing church/school relationships and creating further opportunities to develop links. Both volunteers and teachers noticed that the children's 'chatting and talk was really very spiritual'.

From teacher and volunteer responses, offering a whole day rather than individual lessons brought considerably more flow in the children's learning, and, through immersion in one shared event, had a powerful impact on both schools. This resulted in a better understanding of the story and more in-depth learning.

The whole-day event enabled pupils to make connections and learn the value of reflecting, and was more engaging and enjoyable for teachers, volunteers and children than separate lessons. It also engendered community ethos in the classroom and school. The pilot studies show that the integrated learning event approach led to children understanding the story and its spiritual elements more fully and making more connections. Teachers referred to the depth of learning, from a 'deeper understanding of the story' to thinking 'more deeply' or having 'more empathy for the story'. This deeper learning built as the day went on, so that children changed what they said and how they worked, and it continued after the event, as children were 'quicker to get into that zone of being able to share and talk and think deeply' and had more 'confidence to speak out about how they feel, and to share their opinions and their beliefs and their values'. The results from the children, where they were given specific time to reflect, produced valuable insights for the teachers as well as some assessment material.

The journey day improved links between RE and other areas of the curriculum. It successfully provided resources for some professional development in RE through improved subject knowledge and skills and raised teachers' confidence. It acted as a vehicle to improve weakness in the teaching of Christianity in particular. The learning event and associated pack promoted pupils' spiritual development effectively by allowing for more genuine investigation into and reflection on the implications of religion and belief for their personal lives. It also provided the opportunity to welcome visitors into school. Many of the key indicators for good cross-curricular learning were achieved.

One school used the opportunity to try new models for collective worship, with three different styles, three different ways of seating the children, and different people being involved in delivering them. Teachers felt that the collective worship was 'crucial to the ethos of the day', bringing the whole school together and providing opportunities for participation.

The findings show very clearly that teachers felt that the material contributed to children's RE skills, knowledge and understanding at the same time as enabling good cross-curricular learning to take place and broadening the curriculum.

Church volunteers' point of view

Church volunteers felt that they learnt with the children and that it helped them to think creatively about how to bring a discussion of faith and the Christian story to the children. They felt that it was a 'revelation to hear the children talking about their faith' and a 'wonderful way to combine discussions (of faith) with a practical approach to faith'. One commented that it was 'inspiring, and, in our supposedly secular world, reassuring and touching to see children spiritually and creatively engaged'.

Church volunteers seemed also to have gained some skills and knowledge from the day as they began to suggest that 'we could do something similar to what we did on the journey day' at planning meetings for Christian holiday clubs and family services.

All findings from both schools show that teachers and church volunteers alike felt that this was a positive experience in terms of school and church working together and that it added significantly to the value of the event. They felt that it built relationships between school and church and would continue to do so. Both churches held family services which built on, used and celebrated some of the work done in the journey days.

themselves, the photographs, the comments, the questionnaires. I feel very privileged to have been able to do it. It will go down as one of my things that I remember when I'm old and looking back. It was a very special day.'

Feedback from the pilot sessions

- 'The preparation meeting and the pack together gave you essentially everything you need.'
- 'The material in the scheme of work made a huge difference to preparation and gave us confidence to pass it on, and we knew there was more to it than just the Bible story again.'
- 'The day raised confidence in that type of teaching and learning.'
- Most teachers felt that the scheme of work had everything they needed. They valued the range of workshops, the opportunity to choose workshops and the way the children and day were organised. They felt that it was inspiring and a good starting point for further learning. 'I thought it was fabulous'; it was 'definitely worth it'.
- The difference the scheme of work made to teachers was that it was 'inspiring' and the day looked 'perfectly possible because of the nature of the material… everything is so comprehensive, but isn't prescriptive'.
- The whole day brought power to the learning and gave the children time to really think about it and to produce something of quality without having to move on to something else too quickly. The whole day contributed to the children's 'joy of working'.
- 'First and foremost it was a very creative day… all of the input was very, very, creative and made it very special.'
- One teacher talked about the way the opening 'threaded right the way through to the close' and that this was why they would 'think every day should be like this'. Although they found it difficult to put into words, they felt a 'spirituality running through it and a calmness that was just quite lovely'. Another said that it was not merely a 'retelling of a story; there was more depth to it'.
- Coming together at the beginning and end of the day was significant. It unified a large group of people and 'created community' because they all knew 'what each other had been doing and… why we were doing it'.
- 'It brings it alive, and to those who are perhaps a little doubtful about it, it also shows the huge value. You can't help but see it in the children's work,

UNIT 1

Stepping out on the journey

Bible focus
Matthew 14:22–33

Programme for the day

9.00–9.30am	Whole-school introduction to the day
9.30–10.35am	Workshop 1
10.35–10.55am	Break
10.55–12.00	Workshop 2
12.00–1.00pm	Lunch
1.00–1.15pm (or next day)	'My Journey' reflection
1.15–2.20pm	Workshop 3
2.20–2.30pm	Break
2.30–3.00pm	Whole-school worship

Preparation

Plan a time of reflection on the theme for the staff, governors and church volunteers.

Display a series of photographs of footprints, either as a PowerPoint presentation or set out around the room. Spend some moments looking at the pictures while some quiet music is played (for example, by Moya Brennan, Enya, Taizé, Simeon and John). Then listen to the words of the famous poem 'Footprints in the sand', or the song 'Footprints in the sand' by Leona Lewis.

Together, reflect on the following questions.

- I wonder how you respond to the idea that God supports us through all our experiences in life whatever happens?
- I wonder when you have felt supported?
- How do you feel about the journey ahead of you this year or this term?
- Where are you on your journey?
- What helps you to step out, to try something new?
- What gives you courage?

Conclude the reflection with a time of silence or listen to some quiet music. Then read the following verses aloud.

'In the wilderness… you saw how the Lord your God carried you, as a father carries his son, all the way you went until you reached this place.'
DEUTERONOMY 1:31 (NIV)

I am convinced that neither death nor life, neither angels nor demons, neither the present nor the future, nor any powers, neither height nor depth, nor anything else in all creation, will be able to separate us from the love of God that is in Christ Jesus our Lord.
ROMANS 8:38–39 (NIV)

May the road rise up to meet you, may the wind be always at your back, may the sun shine warm upon your face, the rains fall soft upon your fields, and, until we meet again, may God hold you in the palm of his hand. Amen
IRISH BLESSING

Whole-school introduction to the day

Set up a focal point to include a bowl of water, some pebbles, shells, scented candles, sand, cloth with sea patterns, blue and green fabrics, a cross, and a wild goose or fish symbol. The focal point can be used later to make a reflection corner in school or church.

For ideas for creating reflection corners, see the *Pause for Reflection* pack.

Show pictures of a calm sea accompanied by tranquil music and seashore sounds. If possible, light a scented candle that smells of the seaside. You could have bowls of sand for the children to feel as they enter the hall. Invite the children to share ideas about feelings.

Listen to someone else's response by reading a poem about being next to the sea, and show pictures of a stormy sea accompanied by stormy music and crashing waves. See, for example, the *Values for Life* disk available from Gloucester Diocese (web link on page 94).

Listen to someone else's response by reading a poem about being out in a storm, such as 'Sea Fever' by John Masefield.

Explain that everyone will come back together at the end of the day to share what they have found out.

Workshop 1: Exploring the story

This workshop consists of one engagement followed by a choice of responses with reflections. You could set up between two and four of the different responses.

Learning intention

Children will look at the key feelings of Peter, Jesus and the disciples at different points in the story, and explore the meaning for themselves and for Christians.

Engagement

Read the story from a Bible written for your children's age group (see page 11 for suggestions).

As a class or group, plot a feelings graph for each of the key characters, with emotions on the y axis and time or events in the story on the x axis. Discuss how the themes of the story could help the children, and how the story helps present-day Christians to live their lives today.

For response, select from the following workshop choices (1A to 1J).

Workshop 1A (Curriculum link: Art)

Response

Be inspired by different artists' interpretations of the story. Look at He Qi art—for example, 'Peace, be still' (see gallery web link on page 94). Make sure the children see that this is a painting of a different story, but that the picture includes some of the elements they will need—a boat, the sea, Jesus and the disciples. Alternatively, look at 'In stillness' from the 'Creation' series by McCrimmons (web link on page 94). Notice how the artist has used colour and shape to represent water and peacefulness.

Create a drawing, painting or collage in the style of one of the artists to represent the story and its meaning for the children and for Christians.

Reflection

Invite children to share with the class how and why they have used colour and shape to represent the meaning of the story.

Workshop 1B (Curriculum link: Art, DT, Literacy)

Response

Make a boat from card, paper or junk. Ask the children to write prayers or thoughts on themes from the story, such as fear, trust, support, recognition, hope or the unknown, and add them to the boat's sail, net or anchor, deciding which location is most appropriate for the theme they have chosen.

Reflection

Share some of the prayers and thoughts and talk about what it would be like to be on a boat.

Workshop 1C (Curriculum link: Literacy)

Response

Write a haiku poem (17 syllables in lines of 5, 7 and 5 syllables) that conveys the themes of the story, such as Peter's experience and feelings.

Reflection

Share the poems with the class and talk about how they would have felt if they had been Peter or one of the disciples.

Workshop 1D (Curriculum link: Science)

Response

Explore floating and sinking with different objects, including, if appropriate, the boats you've made, linking to the themes in the story.

Reflection

While they are experimenting with objects floating and sinking, engage the children in conversations about Peter's feelings by asking wondering questions such as 'I wonder how he felt when he was sinking/when he walked on the water?'

Workshop 1E (Curriculum link: Thinking skills)

Response

Generate open-ended questions that you would like to ask somebody from the story, in order to reflect on the story and understand its meaning and significance—

Unit 1 – Stepping out on the journey

such as 'I wonder what made you step out of the boat? How was your life changed after this experience? Did it have an impact on the rest of your life? Why didn't you step out of the boat with Peter?' This could be a whole-class or group exercise.

Write questions on the board, a large piece of paper or sticky notes, depending on the age group. Provide adult help for younger children.

Reflection

Wonder together whether you can use your own experience or knowledge to answer any of the questions.

Workshop 1F
(Curriculum link: Guided reflection)

Response

Ask the children to sit quietly in a comfortable position with their eyes closed. Retell the story as if they are present at the event, including description involving the senses, such as the feel of the spray as the boat goes through the water. Allow pauses for the children to imagine the scene. Before they open their eyes at the end of the story, bring the children back to the room and the here and now.

Reflection

Encourage the children to share their responses—for example, what they saw, how it felt, how they feel now, and whether it helps them to understand the story. An adult could record these responses.

Workshop 1G
(Curriculum link: Art, Literacy)

Response

Give the children a picture of the story. Ask them to make a drawing of themselves and add it to the picture. In pairs, discuss the feelings and experiences they might have had. For example, what would they notice if they were sitting next to Peter in the boat? What would they think and what would they say?

Reflection

Hot-seat some of the children and make a class mind-map of key thoughts and feelings. Wonder together why people's perspectives are different and what influenced the way they felt, depending on where they were in the boat or on the shore, the role they imagined they were in, their own experience and so on.

Workshop 1H
(Curriculum link: Drama, Literacy)

Response

Identify the turning point in the story and then illustrate it through drama—for example, by making a human sculpture or acting out the turning point in small groups.

Reflection

Ask each group to show their ideas, then explain how their drama or sculpture shows the turning point and why they chose that particular point. The 'audience' could give an evaluation, such as three stars ('plus' points) and a wish ('room for improvement' point).

Workshop 1I
(Curriculum link: Thinking skills)

Response

Teach the children how to use PMI using the question, 'Would you want a third arm?' Then use PMI to sort ideas about the story. In groups, children should discuss first of all what they think is good about an idea (five minutes), then what is bad about an idea (five minutes), then what is interesting about an idea (five minutes). They are not allowed to talk about 'minus' points when it is the 'plus' point discussion, and so on. Use PMI to discuss the question, 'Should Peter get out of the boat?' As a class, share responses and decide which is the strongest category (P, M or I).

Reflection

If Peter had known about PMI, would he have made the same decision? Wonder together about what helped him make his decision.

Workshop 1J
(Curriculum link: Literacy)

Response

In pairs, then in fours, then in eights, discuss the following questions. At each stage, choose your best idea to share with the larger group.

- I wonder what Christians would learn from the story?
- I wonder what we can learn?
- I wonder what faith is?

Reflection

Feed back ideas from the questions to the whole class.

Response choices for Foundation Stage and Year 1

For each of the activities, adult helpers, volunteers and LSAs should work with the children to engage them in conversations about the story, the activity, how they would have felt if they'd been there, how the characters might have felt, what we can learn from the story and so on. Choose any of the above responses that may be suitable for this age group, or use the following ideas:

- Wet play: floating and sinking.
- Watching the story on the *Miracle Maker* DVD and talking about it.
- Dressing up as the characters and acting out the story.
- Telling the story with puppets, Playmobil® or small world characters.

Workshop 2: Life is a journey

Learning intention

When Peter made his choice, he drew on his knowledge, experience and skills. It took courage for him to step out of the boat. Where did Peter find his courage? Where do we get courage? Think about the choices we make, what influences or helps us make those choices and what we might therefore need for life's journey.

Engagement

Look at a map or cartoons representing life's decisions, such as 'Road map' by Lat Blaylock (*The Journey of Life and Death*, edited by Joyce Mackley, RE Today), which shows a road of choices and signposts, or the Blob cartoons by Pip Wilson, such as 'Blob Life', 'Blob Journey' or 'Blob Leaps', with associated questions. (See web link, page 94.)

For response, select from the following workshop choices (2A to 2D). For each one, begin by discussing as a class or in pairs what different things (tools) help us in our choices and give us courage for the journey.

Workshop 2A (Curriculum link: Art, Literacy, PSHE)

Response

Pack a suitcase for the journey. Give pairs or individuals an outline of a suitcase or make a 3D suitcase from paper. Think about what you would put in it, such as friendship, love, hope, and either write them on to the suitcase outline or write them on pieces of paper to put into the 3D suitcase.

Children could think of symbols to represent each of the things they would put into the suitcase, such as joined hands for friendship and so on.

Workshop 2B (Curriculum link: Literacy, PSHE)

Response

Write a poem that uses the structure, 'In my pocket I have… the Bible full of God's story which I can use to guide me on my way. In my pocket I have… friends who will cheer me up when I am sad.'

Workshop 2C (Curriculum link: Literacy, PSHE)

Response

Read about the armour of God:

Be ready! Let the truth be like a belt around your waist, and let God's justice protect you like armour. Your desire to tell the good news about peace should be like shoes on your feet. Let your faith be like a shield, and you will be able to stop all the flaming arrows of the evil one. Let God's saving power be like a helmet, and for a sword use God's message that comes from the Spirit. Never stop praying, especially for others. Always pray by the power of the Spirit. Stay alert and keep praying for God's people.

EPHESIANS 6:14–18

Explain that armour serves a purpose, because each piece does a job, a bit like a tool kit. Provide outlines of tools. Alternatively, the children can draw round tools or templates or draw their own tool set. Write on each tool how it would help them to live a good life. For example, an instruction manual could represent the Bible, which guides people through their lives, while a spirit level could represent being balanced.

Unit 1 – Stepping out on the journey

Workshop 2D
(Curriculum link: Literacy, PSHE)

Response

Write a 'recipe', describing the ingredients and method of a good life. It might begin, 'Take two handfuls of courage…'

Reflection

For all four of these workshop activities, share ideas and reflect on the questions: Which are the most common ideas? Which might matter most? Which did Peter have? Which do the children have? How do you find them? Can you learn them?

'My Journey' reflection

Explain to the children that one of the ways God helps people on their journey is by encouraging them to stop and to be still and silent (see, for example, Psalm 46 and Isaiah 30:15). In this spirit, a quiet reflection time has been included in each of the journey days.

Explain to the children that their 'My Journey' book is a special book that they will add to, each time they have a journey day. They need to fill in their name on the front cover, using the label provided (photocopy from page 9 or download from www.barnabasinschools.org.uk/9780857462473). Stick the label to the front cover.

Ask the children to create their own Bible timeline or use the one provided (photocopy from page 9 or download from www.barnabasinschools.org.uk/9780857462473). Stick the Bible timeline on to the first page of the book. On a small piece of paper, draw a picture or symbol to illustrate the story for today (see Matthew 14:22–33), and write the date next to it. Cut this out and stick it on to the timeline.

Ask the children to generate an open or interesting question about the story and write it in their reflection book. Alternatively, ask the children to consider the question, 'I wonder what is the key moment of the story and why it matters?' and write their response in their book. Use scribes if necessary. (It is important that a copy of the child's thoughts is included in the book in order for them to look back on their journey as they progress through the school.) Ask children to share their thoughts with a partner.

This activity can be completed on the day after the workshop.

Workshop 3: Exploring other stories from the Bible

Learning intention

To investigate other stories in the Bible in which God walked with people, each class choosing different stories agreed in advance. Whichever Bible journey is chosen, each class answers the following four key questions:

- Who went on the journey?
- Where did they go?
- I wonder how God helped them?
- I wonder who helps you on your journey through life?

Resources

An online Bible timeline is available (see web link, page 94). Below are suggestions for journeys in the Bible suitable for this activity, which are not covered in other chapters of this book. Reflective storytelling versions of many of them can be found in *The Big Story* by Martyn Payne (Barnabas for Children, 2011), *Godly Play* volumes by Jerome Berryman or *Bible Storybags* and *More Bible Storybags* by Margaret Cooling (Barnabas for Children, 2008 and 2012).

'Testament' is an excellent series of animated Bible stories in a two-DVD boxed set, including Daniel, David and Saul, Moses, Jonah, the Creation and Noah, Elijah, Ruth, Joseph and Abraham. See also the 'What's in the Bible?' collection of DVDs by Phil Vischer and Bible stories on YouTube (check for suitability and download before use).

- Jacob (Genesis 27—29)
- Joseph's various journeys (Genesis 37—43)
- Moses leaving Egypt and travelling through the desert; Joshua taking the people on to the promised land (Exodus and Numbers)
- King David and his loyal friends (2 Samuel 15:14—17:27)
- Daniel (Daniel 1—6)
- Elijah going from Beersheba to Mount Horeb and other journeys (1 Kings 17—21; 2 Kings 1:1–4; 2:1–18)
- Elisha's journeys (2 Kings 4—9; 13:14–21)
- Jonah and the big fish (Jonah 1—4)
- Jesus calms the storm (Luke 8:22–25)
- Jesus and the Samaritan woman (John 4:3–42); the parable of the good Samaritan (Luke 10:25–37)
- The good news is preached in Samaria; Philip and the Ethiopian official (Acts 8:4–40)
- John's journey to Patmos (Revelation 1:9–10)

Engagement (Key Stage 1)

Watch a DVD extract of the chosen Bible story or use a PowerPoint presentation to tell the story (see, for example, 'sermons4kids' web link on page 94) or tell the story using reflective storytelling techniques. Display the key questions above and talk about how we would go about answering them.

Engagement (Key Stage 2)

Compare a painting of your chosen Bible story (from www.joyfulheart.com or www.nationalgallery.org.uk) with the corresponding Bible passage. Display the key questions above or give each group a copy of them and talk about how we would go about answering them.

Response (Key Stages 1 and 2)

The story could be acted out. Answer the key questions for the story you have chosen. Use this information to make a class (KS1) or group (KS2) poster that includes the information you have found out. The poster will be displayed on a school Bible timeline to help other people in the school understand how God walked with people on their Bible journeys.

Engagement (Year 6)

Watch a PowerPoint presentation about faith (see web link, page 94), and talk about what faith might mean to a Christian. As a class, note the key points.

Response

Make a PowerPoint or Photo Story presentation that could be used in a church service or collective worship to show what faith might mean to a Christian. (Photo Story is a Microsoft programme that allows you to arrange pictures, add titles and music and narrate a story.)

Reflection for all choices in Workshop 3

Look at the poster or posters of the story that you've studied and think about the questions the story raises for you. Reflect on how the poster might inspire Christians and others now, and how it might help people to understand how God walked with people on their journeys in the Bible story. I wonder if it inspires you?

Central display

At the end of the workshop, a delegate takes the posters (or Photo Story or PowerPoint presentation on a memory stick) to the school hall and adds them to the whole-school timeline with the help of volunteers from the church.

Whole-school worship

Preparation

As a focal point, create a wall of ideas, with a title banner or border around a board, to reflect the theme 'The Journey of Life', including quotations, pictures, photographs and so on.

Create a display of posters from the workshops. If Year 6 have made PowerPoint or Photo Story presentations, one or more of these could be shown. A child or children from each group or class can share with the school how God helped people in the journey they have studied in Workshop 3.

Show the 'Footprints' PowerPoint presentation, accompanied by quiet music.

Reading

Read the famous 'Footprints in the sand' poem again.

Reflection

Wonder together about who helps us on our journey through life. What gives us courage?

Prayer

Ask children to sit quietly with their eyes closed or looking at a lit candle. Think or pray together about something you want to give thanks for on your journey in life and something you want to ask for help with. You could choose prayers from *The Lion Book of 1000 Prayers for Children* (pages 137–151).

Suggested songs

- One more step along the world I go
- Be thou my vision
- We are walking in the light of God

Blessing

May the road rise up to meet you, may the wind be always at your back, may the sun shine warm upon your face, the rains fall soft upon your fields, and, until we meet again, may God hold you in the palm of his hand. Amen

IRISH BLESSING

Unit 1 extension material

Stepping out on the journey (Foundation Stage)

When the 'Stepping out' unit is not used by the whole school, it is important that Foundation cover this mini-unit before one of the other journey days takes place.

Bible story

Read an appropriate version of the story of Jesus walking on water (Matthew 14:22–33) from *The Barnabas Children's Bible* or *The Big Bible Storybook*. Talk about how Peter, Jesus and the other disciples felt at different points in the story. Act out the story.

Follow-up activities

Choose one of the following activities to explore the story with water play.

- Ice cubes
- Experiment with floating and sinking
- Explore what happens when you make waves
- Float boats (children could make these) with Playmobil® people in them
- Designate the home corner as a boat or make boats from oversized cardboard boxes.

Response

Generate words to describe the sea and the feelings of the disciples; write on wave shapes (in shades of blue) and create a display.

Make bubble prayers by blowing bubbles while thinking of someone you know and praying for them as you pop a bubble.

Listen to sea music and help the children to create their own sea music or accompaniment using rainmakers and so on. They could make their own instruments to produce sea sounds.

Reflect on the story

Wonder together how Peter felt in the boat; how he felt as he stepped out of the boat; when the children have felt like that and who helped them when they felt like that.

Class collective worship

Give children the opportunity to revisit the story, generate questions and ideas from the journey day and add thoughts, questions or responses to their journal.

Reflection

Encourage the children to think about life as a journey. Look at photos, such as a road disappearing into trees, through a gate or up a mountain pass, or a forked road.

Response

Give each child a paper flower shape with six petals. Ask them to write a hope or a prayer for the future in the centre of the flower and then fold down the petals in a clockwise direction to close the flower. Play some quiet music and ask each child in turn to float their folded flowers in a tray or large bowl of water and watch quietly as the petals open. This could be done in a whole-class circle or in a number of smaller groups at tables.

Looking back on the journey

Invite staff, governors and church visitors to reflect on the theme. Think about the story of someone who 'stepped out of the boat', such as Mother Teresa or Martin Luther King. Reflect on some of the experiences from the workshops or any follow-up work that has occurred within school or church.

Response

Give each person a paper flower shape with six petals. In the centre, invite them to write a hope or a prayer for the future. Fold down the petals in a clockwise direction to close the flower. Play some quiet music and take turns to float the folded flowers in a tray or large bowl of water and watch quietly as they open.

Conclude the reflection with a time of silence followed by a blessing such as the Irish one below.

May the road rise up to meet you, may the wind be always at your back, may the sun shine warm upon your face, the rains fall soft upon your fields, and, until we meet again, may God hold you in the palm of his hand. Amen

Unit 1 church-based activity day

This can be a full day, half day or after-school club session.

Setting the scene

Create a focal point with a bowl of water, pebbles, shells, scented candles, sand, cloth or paper or card backdrop with sea patterns or blue and green fabrics, and the wild goose or fish symbol. If you have media facilities, you could show pictures of a calm sea accompanied by tranquil music and seashore sounds.

Provide a Bible timeline such as *The Big Bible Storybook Timeline*. Read the story of Jesus walking on the water.

Suggested activities

Set up one or more of the following activity tables.

- Discuss the words of a creed used by the church and talk about how we could write a creed suitable for an all-age worship service. As individuals or in groups, write a version of the creed, beginning with the words, 'I believe in…' Provide paper, pens, pencils, crayons, and various versions of the creed.
- Talk together about how it feels both to offer and receive the Peace. Make paper chains of people sharing the Peace.
- Make a boat using origami, 3D junk or painting.
- Make a seascape to display the boats when they are finished.
- Try floating the boats you have made. Talk about how God protects people and how faith gives them courage.
- Make jelly seas and edible boats for the 'feast', such as a pear with rice paper sails on cocktail sticks.
- Make a mini orienteering trail round the hall with parts of Peter's story to collect at each point. Margaret Silf writes about our 'inner compass', where due north is when we are true to ourselves, listening and being still with God (see *Landmarks: An Ignatian journey*, DLT, 1998, or *On Making Choices*, Lion Hudson, 2004). Discuss when we might need to trust our inner compass, and how it might help us.
- Make bracelets using beads with different colours, words or shapes as symbols to remind you of what you need or want for your journey—for example, red for love, clear for clear thoughts, arrow for directions and so on. Show examples you have made earlier. (An internet search for Lutheran prayer beads and the 'story of faith' bracelets will give you ideas.)
- Drip paint on to a sheet of paper or card and then blow bubbles in it through a straw. Alternatively, blow bubbles using straws in a dish of soapy water with blue paint in it. Place paper on top to get a print of the bubbles. Use the prints as part of the backdrop for the scene or water collage.
- Place paint in shallow trays lined with thin sponge (scrap stores are a good source). Ask the children to stand gently in the trays and then make a print of their foot on rolls or large sheets of paper.
- Using lining wallpaper, provide a prayer wall or graffiti board in the shape of a boat and some pens for children to write up prayer requests.
- Explore the story of Peter through drama or freeze frame, or explore the story of someone else who has stepped out of the boat (see below).
- Try out some of the ideas in *On Making Choices* by Margaret Silf.

Share food together and say or sing a grace.

Worship

Include a song, prayer and story about someone who has 'stepped out of the boat', such as Mother Teresa or Martin Luther King. Teach a song for all-age worship from the suggested list (see page 20). Read prayers from the graffiti wall or light some candles in front of it and spend time together looking at the different prayers and praying quietly.

UNIT 2

Creation: a perfect relationship

Bible focus
Genesis 1:1—2:4

Programme for the day

9.00–9.30am	Whole-school introduction to the day
9.30–10.35am	Workshop 1
10.35–10.55am	Break
10.55–12.00	Workshop 2
12.00–1.00pm	Lunch
1.00–1.15pm (or next day)	'My Journey' reflection
1.15–2.20pm	Workshop 3
2.20–2.30pm	Break
2.30–3.00pm	Whole-school worship

Preparation

Plan a time of reflection on the theme for staff, governors and church volunteers. Have music playing, such as the Planets Suite by Holst, the Pastoral Symphony by Beethoven, 'Memory of Trees', 'Watermark' or 'Paint the Sky with Stars' by Enya, or 'The Moldeau' by Smetana.

Place photographs of beautiful examples of creation on tables, including large and small scale. Invite people to wander between them and stop when one catches their eye. Invite people to think about why it caught their eye, how it makes them feel, and what it reminds them of. Does it inspire them?

Listen to a version of the song 'What a wonderful world'. Give each person some playdough and invite them to model something while they listen to the music and think about what it is like to create something.

Conclude the reflection with a time of silence or more quiet music followed by these verses from Psalm 104.

Praise the Lord, my soul.
Lord my God, you are very great;
you are clothed with splendour and majesty…
He makes springs pour water into the ravines;
it flows between the mountains.
They give water to all the beasts of the field;
the wild donkeys quench their thirst.
The birds of the sky nest by the waters;
they sing among the branches.
He waters the mountains from his upper chambers;
the land is satisfied by the fruit of his work.
He makes grass grow for the cattle,
and plants for people to cultivate—
bringing forth food from the earth:
wine that gladdens human hearts,
oil to make their faces shine,
and bread that sustains their hearts…
How many are your works, Lord!
In wisdom you made them all;
the earth is full of your creatures.

PSALM 104:1–2, 10–15, 24 (NIV)

Whole-school introduction to the day

Explore the setting of the story through the senses. Make a creation focal point with globes, maps, plants, flowers and so on. Show pictures of aspects of creation that you used in the preparatory reflection above, on PowerPoint or whiteboard, with background music such as 'For the beauty of the earth' by John Rutter or 'Indescribable' by Chris Tomlin.

Engagement

Mix two cups of flour with half a cup of salt. Add quarter of a cup of hand-hot water, knead to make a salt dough, then create an object. Tell the Christian story of creation using a creative storytelling method. See, for example, 'Reflect-a-Story: Christian creation' by TTS (web link on page 94), *Godly Play Volume 2* or *More Bible Storybags*.

Read Psalm 8 with music playing in the background. Highlight that God had a special relationship with Adam and Eve (he walked with them in the garden of Eden, Genesis 3:8). Explain that Christians aim to get back to that special relationship with God in which they understand that God is with them all the time.

Sing the song 'Sing to the Music Maker' together.

(Fischy Music). Explain that everyone will return to the hall at the end of the day to share and celebrate what they have discovered about God's creation. Before children go to their workshops, ask God's blessing on the day, using the words, 'The earth is the Lord's and everything in it. Amen'.

Use the focal point objects and pictures and draped fabric to make a reflection corner. For examples of reflection corners, see the *Pause for Reflection* pack.

Workshop 1: Be creative

Workshop 1A (Curriculum link: Art)

Learning intention

Christians believe that looking at the wonder of creation helps them to understand something of the nature of God. Children begin to raise questions about the world and its origins and consider their own and other people's viewpoints.

Engagement

Look at examples of art that uses pointillism, such as Seurat's paintings (see web links on page 94). Look at photos of close-up views of nature such as a butterfly's wing or a piece of rock. You could use an electronic microscope attached to the whiteboard.

Response

Using the technique of pointillism, create a close-up view of something in the natural world. Link it to the idea that everything in the world is made out of atoms. You could take shaped pieces of paper, such as circles, then frame a circle on the picture or object and enlarge the picture on to the paper circle using pointillist technique. Provide paints or pens in a good range of colours to enable shading.

Reflection

In the Bible it says that when God created the world, he saw that it was good (Genesis 1:31). Wonder together about how children feel when they look at something beautiful in nature. Wonder together about whether looking at nature helps us to think about God.

Workshop 1B (Curriculum link: Art)

Learning intention

Children experience what it is like to create something and reflect on their feelings about being a creator. They make links between their experience and Christian belief in God as a creator.

Engagement

Look at the range of natural materials used in art (see web links, page 94). Ask the children the following wondering questions.

- I wonder what you notice about the pictures?
- I wonder what you think about how the artist has chosen and used their materials?
- I wonder what difference it makes that the materials used are natural and then displayed outside as part of nature?

Response

Produce a piece of art using natural objects. Choose from the following, offering choice within the workshop if desired.

- Leaf prints or Japanese hammered leaf prints
- Collage of natural objects
- Clay, to represent forming objects out of the dirt
- A piece of art to be displayed outside in the school grounds, perhaps in a spiritual garden

For Japanese hammered leaf prints, you will need flowers or leaves in bright colours, not too wet and not too dry; watercolour or other rough, acid-free paper; a selection of hammers (special ball-peen or cross-peen hammers work best, but ordinary hammers will do); a hard work surface such as a cutting board or slab of wood; paper towels; tweezers or cocktail sticks.

Place the paper on a board. Trim the flowers or leaves and lay them flat on the paper, covering them with a few sheets of paper towel. Carefully draw round the edge of the leaf or flower so that you know where to hammer. Hammer in rows up and down and then across to ensure that you have hammered each part of the object. Peel the paper towels away to check that you have done enough hammering. Peel the leaf or flower off the paper using tweezers.

Reflection

Wonder together in what ways the children are pleased with what they have created. Wonder together if they would do anything differently another time and how God felt when he had finished creating the world.

Workshop 1C (Curriculum link: Art)

Learning intention

The children consider the question, 'If God were an artist, how would he paint the world?' through looking at artists' interpretations of creation and God as a creator.

Engagement

Choose from the following options (you could choose more than one).

Show pictures or video clips of creation, or make your own PowerPoint slide show with similar images. Alternatively, show pupils a range of children's interpretations of God in various styles and media, such as from Spirited Arts, or show McCrimmons' 'Behold' poster or 'Creation' banner (web links, page 94), or use the art in *Picturing Creation* (RE Today).

Ask the following wondering questions.

- I wonder how this presentation or art helps us think about what Christians believe about God as a creator?
- I wonder how it might inspire them?
- I wonder how it might inspire you?

Response

Either in pairs or as a group, make a PowerPoint presentation to reflect the theme, or paint God as an artist creating the world. Alternatively, ask children to imagine themselves being 'God the artist' and produce a display of their work. Various techniques could be used, such as producing a gallery of pictures, displaying found objects, collage, a quilt of ideas and so on.

Reflection

- Wonder together if thinking about God as an artist helps us understand what it might be like to create the world.
- Wonder if the children take more care of something if they have made it themselves.
- Wonder if they would take more care of the world if they believed that God had created it.

Workshop 1D (Curriculum link: Drama and Dance)

Learning intention

Encourage the children to identify key themes in the Christian creation story and respond through dance and drama.

Engagement

Recap the story and then discuss key themes and opportunities for repetition, such as when God 'saw that it was good' at the end of each day. Listen to a piece of music that you have chosen to represent the process of creation. Discuss how it makes the children feel, the mood and atmosphere the composer has created and so on.

Response

Choreograph and perform a creation dance. Groups could take a section each. Write the choreography down as a line with symbols or annotation on long strips of paper. (This work could be extended by thinking about costumes and props.)

Reflection

After each performance, ask each group, 'I wonder how you feel about the dance you created?' Ask everyone else to award three stars and a wish (three things they liked and one thing that could be improved).

Workshop 1E (Curriculum link: Music)

Learning intention

Pupils will learn that art and music can be used to retell the story of creation and its significance to Christians, explore what it is like to create something using the medium of music, and reflect on their own feelings.

Engagement

Choose stunning photographs to represent each of the days of creation or use art from McCrimmons, Sophie Hacker, or *Picturing Creation* (from RE Today, including CD-Rom). Show the pictures on the whiteboard.

Response

Make available printed versions of pictures or art for each day of creation. As a class or in groups, create musical pictures of each of the days of creation using a range of percussion instruments. Each group could create music for one day or for all seven days.

Reflection

Perform the music as the pictures are shown. Ask, 'I wonder how you felt as the music was played? Did it fully reflect the story or the picture?'

Workshop 2: Be communicative

Workshop 2A (Curriculum link: Thinking and questioning)

Learning intention

Pupils explore the Christian belief that humans are stewards of creation. They then consider in what sense they think of themselves as stewards.

Engagement

Show pictures of the earth from the moon and, if desired, read quotes from some of the first astronauts who saw the world from this point of view.

Response

Christians believe that human beings are stewards of creation. Explore this belief in one of the following ways.

- Foundation Stage, Years 1 and 2: Read *Wonderful Earth* by Nick Butterworth and debate the question, 'I wonder how we can look after the earth?'
- Years 2 and 3: Diamond-sort important statements about what Christians believe about creation and their responsibility to care for it. Use statements from the list below, or create your own. Record the sorting results with a camera.
- Key Stage 2: Diamond-sort important statements about what Christians believe about creation and their responsibility to care for it, then write ten rules for caring for creation. Use statements from the list below, or create your own.
- Year 6: Debate the statement, 'To look after creation is the most important thing a Christian can do.' Vote as a class on the statement: For, Against and Abstain. Divide the class into an even number of small groups and allocate half in favour and half against. Tell each group to nominate one person to be the speaker. Give the groups statements and facts to look at. Give them about five minutes to formulate their ideas. Ask groups in turn to speak in favour and then against (for two minutes each), then open the debate to the floor. Ask one person to summarise the arguments for the motion and another the arguments against the motion. Take a second vote.

Suggested diamond-sort statements are as follows.

- The Bible tells Christians that they are stewards of creation (Genesis 1:28; Psalm 8:6).
- Christians must care for their animals (Proverbs 12:10).
- Christians believe they have to look after the world and everything in it (Genesis 2:15–20).
- God created the world, so we should look after it.
- The world is special.
- Christians should use solar power.
- Christians should plant trees.
- Christians should eat organic food.
- Christians should be careful how they use electricity.
- Christians should not drop litter.
- Christians should support a charity that looks after God's world.
- Christians should recycle as much as possible.

Reflection

In pairs, think about how we can care for the earth.

Workshop 2B (Curriculum link: Literacy)

Learning intention

Children will reflect upon the significance of each aspect ('day') of creation and think about their inter-dependence. They will think about how this may be symbolised.

Engagement

Tell the story using either *The Big Story*, *Godly Play Volume 2*, *More Bible Storybags* or 'Reflect-a-Story: Christian creation' (TTS). Discuss with the children what is special about each day of creation, and think about the symbols chosen to represent each day in your chosen storytelling method, such as the 3D pieces in 'Reflect-a-Story'.

Response

Having retold the creation story, divide the children into six groups. Ask each group to design a card or plaque to represent one of the days of creation, and use these to tell the story again. Each group needs to be able to say what is special about their day and think about what life would be like if that day had never been made.

Reflection

Sit in a circle and tell the story using the children's plaques. When it is their turn, each group explains their thoughts and ideas. Ask, 'I wonder what is special about your day? I wonder what it would be like without your day?'

Workshop 2C (Curriculum link: Literacy)

Learning intention

Children reflect upon the significance of each aspect ('day') of creation and think about their interdependence. They think about how this may be symbolised.

Engagement

Read 'The creation' from *God's Trombone*, a collection of poems by James Weldon Johnson. Ask, 'I wonder how the author has used instruments to help him imagine how God created the world?'

Response

Ask pupils to work in pairs to add their own extra verse to the poem, based on a different instrument from the ones that James Johnson has used, such as a rainstick, violin, bagpipes and so on. If desired, have pictures of instruments to show the children, or audio clips of the sounds that they make.

Reflection

Sit in a circle to read out the verses the children have written. When it is their turn, each group explains their thoughts and ideas. Ask, 'I wonder if the instrument chosen makes a different interpretation or adds a new dimension to God's creating?'

Workshop 2D (Curriculum link: Art, Literacy)

Learning intention

Children reflect upon the feelings associated with creation and upon the Christian understanding of the nature of God as creator.

Engagement

Read Paul Bunday's poem 'In the beginning…':

In the beginning… God laughed…
And earth was glad.
The sound of the laughter
Was like the swaying and swinging of thunder
  in mirth;
Like the rush of the north on a drowsy and
  dozing land;
It was cool. It was clear.
The lion leapt down
At the bleating feet of the frightened lamb and smiled;
And the viper was tamed by the thrill of the earth,
At the holy laughter.
We laughed, for the Lord was laughing with us
  in the evening;
For the laughter of love went pealing into the night;
And it was good.

Alternatively, read the Wellspring Creation Liturgy or look at calligraphy, including examples where the first letter of a word is illuminated (see web links, page 94).

Response

Ask pupils to write their own poem or liturgy in the same style as Paul Bunday or the Wellspring Liturgy and present it using calligraphy (there may only be time to use calligraphy for the first letter or line of the poem).

Reflection

Ask some wondering questions:

- I wonder if you can think of a time when you laughed because something was so good or so beautiful?
- I wonder if God laughed when he saw that the world was good?
- I wonder if calligraphy can help you understand ideas?

Workshop 2E (Curriculum link: Literacy, Thinking skills)

Learning intention

Children reflect upon the feelings associated with creation and upon the Christian understanding of the nature of God as creator.

Engagement

If not used previously, tell the story of creation from the version found in *Godly Play Volume 2* or *More Bible Storybags*.

Response

Explore the wondering questions that are provided at the end of the story in the book you have chosen. Provide a variety of art materials with which the children can make a free response to the ideas, wondering and experience of the story.

Reflection

The reflection takes place as part of the storytelling.

'My Journey' reflection

Complete the 'My Journey' reflection book during this session or during the next school day. Show the children a lily and then read Matthew 6:25–29. Explain that Jesus used the example of a lily to explain how much God cares. Ask, 'If you were to choose something really beautiful in creation, what would it be?' Alternatively, older children could consider which is more beautiful, something from nature or something man-made.

On a small piece of paper, ask the children to draw a picture or symbol to illustrate creation, write the date next to it, and then cut out and stick the picture or symbol on to the timeline in their 'My Journey' book. Generate an open or interesting question about the story and write it in the reflection book. Use scribes if necessary (it is important that a copy of the child's thoughts is included in the book in order for them to see their journey). Ask children to share their thoughts with a partner.

Workshop 3: Be knowledgeable

Workshop 3A
(Curriculum link: Science, Numeracy)

Learning intention

Children notice patterns in creation and reflect upon their feelings and upon the Christian understanding of the nature of God as creator. They raise questions about the world, how they appreciate beauty and how Christians appreciate beauty.

Engagement

Look at photographs of snowflakes. Explore Kepler's findings about snowflakes and individuality (see web links on page 94).

Ask, 'I wonder how you feel, looking at the snowflakes close up?'

Response

Make snowflakes from paper. Fold a square in half. Then, from the centre of the folded edge, fold the two sides in at an angle of 60 degrees. Cut round the open edges to make an arc shape, and cut out sections to form a snowflake pattern when the paper is unfolded.

The snowflake looks particularly effective when different sizes of cut-out sections are made. The more pieces of paper are cut out and the smaller they are, the more intricate the pattern produced.

Reflection

Ask, 'I wonder what you feel when you look at the snowflake you have created?'

Workshop 3B
(Curriculum link: Science, Numeracy)

Learning intention

Children notice patterns in creation and reflect upon their feelings and upon the Christian understanding of the nature of God as creator. They raise questions about the world, how they appreciate beauty and how Christians appreciate beauty.

Engagement

Show children the beginning of the Fibonacci sequence (0, 1, 1, 2, 3, 5) and see whether they notice the pattern and can predict the next numbers. You could differentiate by giving children more or less of the sequence.

Explain what the Fibonacci sequence is and how it is expressed throughout nature. For background information and examples to share with the children, see the web links on page 94. There are also PowerPoint presentations about the sequence to be found on YouTube.

Response

Draw a spiral formed from Fibonacci numbers. Start by drawing a 1cm square with another 1cm square below it, then 2cm, 3cm and so on. Add a sequence of increasing squares, moving counter-clockwise. Once you have filled a large piece of paper, start from one of the smallest squares and draw quarter circles inside the squares to form a spiral. (See diagram below, downloadable from www.barnabasinschools.org.uk/9780857462473.)

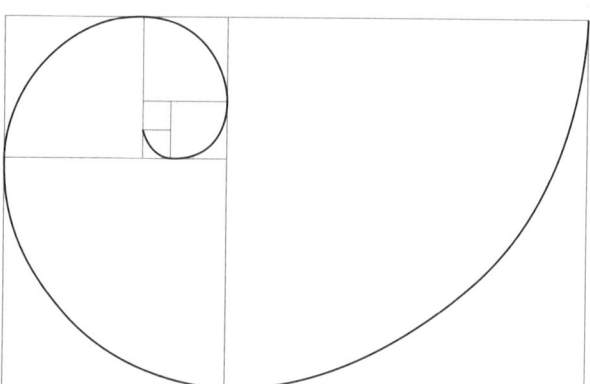

To fit on more squares, use a scaled-down version: for example, draw squares of 0.5cm, 0.5cm, 1cm, 1.5cm and so on, or 0.2cm, 0.2cm, 0.4cm, 0.6cm and so on.

Alternatively, draw an example of a Fibonacci spiral from nature, such as a sunflower, romano cauliflower, sea shell, ram's horn, wave breaking, or galaxy.

Reflection

Ask wondering questions as follows.

- I wonder how you feel about these patterns that can be found in nature, from tiny shells to galaxies?
- I wonder if this changes your ideas about how Christians see God as a creator?
- I wonder if it changes your ideas about God as a creator?

Workshop 3C
(Curriculum link: Science, Art)

Learning intention

Children raise questions about the world, how they appreciate beauty and how Christians appreciate beauty.

Engagement

Read Psalm 24:1–2 and then go on a senses walk to take nature photographs, or look at a selection of photographs from nature.

Generate wondering questions to make a photo-and-question wall about creation as seen in the school grounds or local area. Talk about what feelings the children have when they look at nature on the walk and when they look at the photographs. Talk about how looking carefully and consciously could help Christians to appreciate the beauty of God's created world in their own locality rather than in faraway places that are often shown when we talk about the beauty, awe and wonder of God's creation, such as mountains or massive waterfalls.

Response

Print photographs or view images on computers. In groups or pairs, write questions and thoughts on sticky notes or thought bubbles (use a scribe for younger or lower-ability writers). Questions might include, 'What do you notice about it? What makes it different? Why did you choose it?' Display the photographs and captions in the hall for the whole-school worship later.

Reflection

Using a whiteboard, share some of the photographs and captions with the whole class. Ask, 'I wonder how you feel when you look at nature?'

Workshop 3D
(Curriculum link: Science, Art)

Learning intention

Children explore interesting and mysterious perspectives on the world and life in the world and think about how these influence their own and other people's understanding of creation.

Engagement

Look at images of the earth from space, or listen to Neil Armstrong's comments when he saw the earth from space. Look at Google Earth, 'The nine planets', a multimedia tour that inspires awe and wonder. Look at the 'Earth from above' photo collection by Yann Arthus-Bertrand (see web links, page 94). Then use a search engine to find photographs taken through the electron microscope.

Discuss how none of these views could have been seen by humans before the 20th century. How is our perception or view of the world changed when we look from these different perspectives?

Response

Give each group copies of pictures of space and the earth from the air, and electron microscope photos.

In groups or pairs, make mind maps (see Google Images 'mind maps' for many examples) to explore the idea of seeing the earth from different perspectives; include facts, feelings and spiritual ideas. Three arms could be about the examples above (views from space and from above the earth, and micro-views).

As an extension, think about other perspectives—for example, a religious point of view (the idea that all the earth is sacred), how the earth was formed, or stewardship of the earth.

Reflection

Look at the Blob World cartoon from the *Little Book of Blob Questions* by Pip Wilson and Ian Long (see www.lulu.com). Reflect on the following questions.

- I wonder what you think this picture is about?
- I wonder how it relates to other ways of looking at the world?
- I wonder where God is?

- I wonder where you would like to be?
- I wonder which blob confuses you… surprises you… you feel like… concerns you most… and why?

Alternatively, share ideas from mind maps with the class (especially ideas about spiritual or religious perspectives).

Whole-school worship

Preparation

Helpers will have brought lots of examples of art to provide or add to the focal point. Project a slideshow of pictures from workshops, with music such as 'For the beauty of the earth' (John Rutter), as children come in. Alternatively, play 'Almighty God' by Tim Hughes with a slideshow of photographs from creation. Share special moments from the day from each class or workshop.

Reading

Ask your 'Open the Book' team, if you have one in your school, to share the creation story from *Open the Book Handbook* Year 1, complete with prayers and reflection. Alternatively, use the following reading by Amergin, an early first-century Celtic prince.

I am the wind which breathes upon the sea,
I am the wave of the ocean,
I am the murmur of the billows,
I am the ox of the seven combats,
I am the vulture upon the rocks,
I am the beam of the sun,
I am the fairest of plants,
I am the wild boar in valour,
I am a salmon in the water,
I am the lake in the plain,
I am a word of knowledge,
I am the point of the lance in battle,
I am the God who created the fire of thought.
Who is it that throws light into the meeting of the
 mountains?
Who tells the ages of men,
Who points to the sun's resting place, if not I?

FROM THE *LEABHAR GABHALA BOOK OF INVASIONS*
(TRADITIONAL, ELEVENTH CENTURY)

Reflection

Look at the pictures and think about all the amazing things in creation that the children have studied today—some right under their noses, others as far away as we can see with a space telescope. Reflect for a few moments on how amazing it is that we can see all these things and know about them, and how beautiful and awesome they are.

Prayer

You have told us, Lord, that we are the stewards of your creation and that it is up to people to care for the whole earth. We ask you to help us remember to do that in little as well as big ways—by caring for animals, picking up litter, turning off a light, or planting a garden. Amen

More prayers can be found in *The Lion Book of 1000 Prayers for Children* (pages 275–296 and 321–351).

Suggested songs

This is the day
Jesus is Lord
How great thou art
Great is thy faithfulness
Great in power (by Russell Fragar) (downloadable from www.musicnotes.com)

Blessing

Praise God, from whom all blessings flow;
Praise him, all creatures here below;
Praise him above, ye heavenly host:
Praise Father, Son, and Holy Ghost.

Unit 2 extension material

Workshop for Foundation Stage

Engagement

Share one of the suggested books below or go on a welly walk and look at nature in the school grounds. Take photographs and note down the children's feelings, comments and questions as they walk around (see Workshop 3C on page 29 for ideas).

Response

Provide a sand tray with lots of animals to show diversity, and talk about the similarities and differences. Provide a water tray with lots of fish and other creatures, or make a mural by creating a background with sky, land and water and asking each child to draw or paint a different creature (including humans), or build up a picture of creation in the air, land and water.

Suitable story books

- *Colourful Creation*, Lucy Moore and Honor Ayres (Barnabas, 2009)
- *Becoming Me: A story of creation*, Martin Boroson and Christopher Gilvan-Cartwright (Frances Lincoln, 2002)
- *Creation Song*, Anna Scott-Brown and Elena Gomez (Lion Hudson, 2008)
- *The Creation Story: In words and sign language*, John P. Audia and David Spohn (Liturgical Press, 2007)
- *Wonderful Earth*, Nick Butterworth and Mick Inkpen (John Hunt, 2010)

Class collective worship

Revisiting the story

Give children the opportunity to revisit the story, generate questions and ideas from the journey day and add thoughts, questions or responses to their journal.

Reflection

Read Psalm 148 and then listen to 'For the beauty of the earth' (traditional or John Rutter version).

Response

If we appreciate creation, we can be inspired to care for it. Think about how we care for creation using the following questions.

- I wonder what we could do as a school?
- I wonder what we could do as a class?
- I wonder what we could do as individuals?

Prayer

For the prayer 'Thank you, God, for the wonders of your creation…' ask the children to suggest ideas, such as 'Thank you, God, for the drop of dew on a spider's web… the crash of a wave as it breaks on the rocks…' and so on. Sum up at the end with, 'Thank you, God, that we can enjoy your creation; help us to notice all the wonderful things around us. Amen'

Alternatively, there are many prayers about creation in *The Lion Book of 1000 Prayers for Children* (pages 275–296 and 321–351).

Looking back on the journey

Plan a time of reflection on the theme for staff, governors and church visitors. Consider the following questions and discuss ways in which the questions are already being addressed.

- If to look after creation (to be stewards of it) is a Christian duty, what could that look like in our church and our school?
- If it is better spiritually to spend time out of doors and to be a part of and notice nature, have we done anything this year to encourage more outdoor work and play at school and church?
- Do our lessons and services celebrate creation?

Talk together about the fact that scientists are finding that the eyesight of some urban children is deteriorating; they can no longer focus on long distances as they spend the majority of their time indoors. See also research done in this field by the National Trust (*50 Things to Do Before You're 11¾*), by Susan Greenfield (*ID: The Quest for Meaning in the 21st Century*) or by Sue Palmer (see web link, page 94).

Discuss what we could do better and how we could implement at least one idea, such as creating a school garden, outdoor school, outdoor services, church family walks (share local knowledge with families), Rogation Sunday services and so on.

Conclude the reflection with a time of silence or quiet music, followed by a closing prayer:

Father, we thank you for this wonderful world and the variety of amazing things in it. Help us to appreciate and care for even the smallest aspect of creation. Help us to make our school and church a place where we all learn about and practise good stewardship. Amen

Alternatively, choose a prayer from eco-congregation resources (see web link, page 94).

Unit 2 church-based activity day

This can be a full day, half day or after-school club session.

Setting the scene

Set up a focal point using objects from nature, or show pictures of nature accompanied by music. Have a Bible timeline on display, such as *The Big Bible Storybook Timeline*.

Tell the story of creation in an interactive way (see *Godly Play Volume 2*, Reflect-a-Story: Christian creation (TTS) or *More Bible Storybags*.

Suggested activities

Day One (day and night)

Look at the creatures that come out in the day and the night, or compare one type in particular, such as moths and butterflies, and note the differences between them. Alternatively, make pictures in black, grey and white, then in colour (photographs or art). Talk about how God is with us day and night, and how he walked with Moses and the people of Israel as they journeyed from Egypt (Exodus 13:21). Think about how we might pray to God differently in the day and the night.

Day Two (sky and water)

Look at different sorts of clouds, find out all about them and produce cloud pictures, or go outside and lie on the ground (take blankets if it's too cold or wet, but don't miss out on the experience). Look at the patterns the clouds make, and talk about how it makes you feel to look at the vastness of the sky, and how it constantly changes.

Look at pictures, listen to sound clips or watch video clips of water in creation, such as streams, rivers, lakes, ponds and sea. Ask, 'I wonder if you know what the link is between clouds and all these examples of water?' Allow the children to offer lots of answers, then talk about how each cloud is made of drops of water and that this happens through the water cycle. There are excellent songs and clips about the water cycle on YouTube. Alternatively, children could make their own versions.

Talk about the vastness of God's love, and the awe and wonder we experience when we think of God. Make individual mind maps, or one large one, of everyone's ideas and experiences. (Do a Google search for images of mind maps to see hundreds of examples.)

Day Three (land and sea plants)

Take children outside to take photographs of nature—detailed close-ups as well as pictures of whole plants. Make a gallery of prints if you have a printer, or a rolling slideshow on a computer. (This could be used in worship.) Alternatively, plant seedlings, create a vegetable plot (pots work well if you can't use a piece of ground), or sow cress. You could also make a miniature 'garden' or 'nature' scene (rather like an Easter garden, or one for the local flower show) for the worship. (You could make individual gardens or one large shared one.) You will need to provide plants and containers (or plates). The children could collect objects to add, such as twigs or pebbles, or you could provide those too.

Talk about how God sustains us with plants as food but also brings us joy through their beauty. Talk about how he teaches us through the life of plants (Matthew 6:28) or think about how plants are mentioned in the Bible, from tiny mustard seeds (Mark 4:30–34) to cedar or fig trees.

Day Four (sun and moon)

Look at photos of the sun and talk about how it sustains life. Make a huge sun from cut-out hands in shades of yellow and orange. Make a moon by collage, with shades of white and silver on a cut-out card outline. Make 3D stars.

Talk about how the earth is in just the right place in relation to the sun and how only a tiny difference would mean that life could not exist on earth. Explain how the moon has an influence on tides, plants and so on. Make sun-, moon- and star-shaped cookies, using the recipe below.

- 100g butter or margarine
- 50g caster sugar
- 175g plain flour

1. Pre-heat oven to 150°C/300°F/Gas 2.
2. Cream the butter or margarine and caster sugar together until the mixture is light and fluffy.

3. Stir in the flour. Once mixed, knead the dough together until it forms a ball. Add a sprinkle of flour if the dough is at all sticky.
4. Place the dough in a plastic bag and chill in the fridge for at least an hour (optional).
5. Roll out the dough on a lightly floured surface until it is about 5mm thick.
6. Cut out the dough using your chosen cutter.
7. Place the biscuits on a baking tray lined with baking parchment and bake in the centre of the oven for 25 minutes or until golden brown.
8. Let the biscuits cool on a wire tray before decorating if you wish.

Day Five (water creatures and flying creatures)

Go pond dipping or bird spotting. Make a mural of water creatures and flying creatures. Write facts, poems or riddles about them. Provide a background with sky, land and water. Talk about the diversity in God's creation.

Day Six (animals and people)

Make pictures and write facts, poems or riddles about land creatures. Add them to the mural if you have made one.

Day Seven (rest)

Set up a quiet reflective area with music (perhaps including nature sounds), pictures from nature and candles. A gazebo or some curtains to separate the area would be helpful. Display the Bible verse: 'By the seventh day God had finished his work, and so he rested' (Genesis 2:2). Talk to the children about how sometimes it is only when we are quiet and at rest that we can really appreciate God's presence around us.

Optional activities

Display a world map, globe or picture of the earth and a basket with blank thought bubbles so that pupils can stick on their thoughts about God's created world, and what they would like to pray for or share with others.

Alternatively, make a creation quilt from paper squares showing the types of things that people enjoy, such as science, art and craft, photography, writing and so on. Make pictures or write poems and find out information about created things in your locality, or do a scientific survey of a square metre in the church grounds and plot everything that you can find living or growing there. Record the weather on the day and make a square full of that information.

Join the squares to make a giant quilt that can be displayed for the worship at the end of this session.

There are lots of ideas available on the internet about being an eco-congregation: see web link on page 94.

Learn songs from Fischy Music, such as 'Down to earth', 'Music maker', or 'Even before I was born'. Share food together, and say or sing a grace.

Worship

Go on a prayer walk, noticing and giving thanks for God's creation.

Use bubble prayers: ask someone to name something from God's creation that they can see, to give thanks for. Then blow bubbles. Each person chooses one bubble to follow and, when that bubble pops, they say 'Amen'. Repeat as many times as desired or each time you pause on your prayer walk.

UNIT 3

Abraham and Sarah's journey

Bible focus

Genesis 12:1–9; 13:1–18
(Abram and Sarai leave Haran)
Genesis 15:1–6 (God's promise to Abram)
Genesis 17:4–5, 15–16
(God changes Abram's and Sarai's names)
Genesis 18:1–15 (The three visitors)
Hebrews 11:1–3, 8–12 (Abraham's great faith)
Matthew 1:1–17 (Jesus' family tree)
Matthew 25:35–36
(Jesus teaches about hospitality)

Programme for the day

9.00–9.30am	Whole-school introduction to the day
9.30–10.35am	Workshop 1
10.35–10.55am	Break
10.55–12.00	Workshop 2
12.00–1.00pm	Lunch
1.00–1.15pm (or next day)	'My Journey' reflection
1.15–2.20pm	Workshop 3
2.20–2.30pm	Break
2.30–3.00pm	Whole-school worship

Preparation

Plan a time of reflection on the theme for the staff, governors and church volunteers. Read the story of God telling Abram and Sarai to leave Haran and travel wherever he would send them (Genesis 12:1–9; 13:1–18). A shortened version suitable for Key Stage 2 can be found in *The Lion Bible for Children* pages 28–32, *The Barnabas Schools Bible* pages 20–22 or *The Lion Children's Bible in 365 Stories*. Looking to the year ahead, ask, 'I wonder what will be familiar? I wonder what is unknown? I wonder how you feel about these two aspects?'

Read how God changed Abram and Sarai's names to symbolise his promises to them and as a sign that they belonged to him (Genesis 17:4–5, 15–16). Names are important and carry significance. When someone tells you their name, they are telling you something very important about themselves and trusting you with it. Listen to 'Facedown' by Matt Redman (download from iTunes or find on YouTube) and think about the following questions as you listen to the music.

- I wonder how you feel when someone uses your name?
- I wonder if it matters how they do it?
- I wonder who you trust your name with?
- I wonder how you show that somebody else can trust you?

If you were given a new name that symbolised where you are on life's journey, what would it be? (You could share ideas and talk about the names you would choose.)

Conclude the reflection with a time of silence or quiet music followed by a blessing such as the one below.

Don't be afraid. I have rescued you. I have called you by name; now you belong to me.
ISAIAH 43:1 (CEV)

Whole-school introduction to the day

Explore the setting of the story through the senses by displaying maps, a sand tray or bag, a compass, and labels saying 'covenant', 'promises', 'faith' and 'name'. Use these elements to make a reflection corner (for ideas, see the *Pause for Reflection* pack). Play music as the children come in, such as 'In the Steppes of Central Asia' by Borodin.

Engagement

Explain that the music is all about a journey. Ask, 'I wonder if you have ever been on a journey to somewhere new? I wonder how you felt before you set off… as you travelled… when you arrived?'

Tell the story of Abraham and Sarah from a children's Bible, *Godly Play Volume 2, More Bible Storybags* or *The Big Story*. If you have an 'Open the Book' team, they could tell the story from Year 1 or show the *Miracle*

Mysteries DVD available from Rhema Resources (see web link, page 94).

Ask, 'I wonder how Abraham and Sarah felt when God asked them to leave Haran? I wonder what it was like on their journey to places they'd never been to?'

Point out that Abraham and Sarah trusted that God was with them and helping them on their journey.

Read the Bible verse, 'With your powerful arm you protect me from every side' (Psalm 139:5).

Prayer

Listen to or say together the following prayer.

Christ beside me, Christ within me
Christ behind me, Christ before me
Christ beneath me, Christ above me…
Christ in heart of all who meet me. Amen

FROM ST PATRICK'S BREASTPLATE

Sing 'We are marching in the light of God' (Siyahamba) as the children go out to learn all about Abraham and Sarah's journey, explaining that they will return at the end of the day to share what they have discovered.

Workshop 1: Be creative

Workshop 1A (Curriculum link: DT)

Learning intention

Children learn about the nomadic journey of Abraham and Sarah, reflecting on the feelings and challenges for Abraham and Sarah and how they might feel themselves if they had to make a similar journey.

Engagement

Read Genesis 12:1–9.

Lead a guided visualisation about camping out in the desert. Show pictures of nomads' tents and the environment that Abraham travelled through. Ask, 'I wonder how you would feel if you slept under the stars? I wonder how you would feel if you slept in a tent? If you were moving into places you'd never been to before, I wonder how you would feel about your tent?' and then generate questions about the human need for shelter.

Response

Design a tent for Abraham and his family to sleep in, using paper, small pegs, glue and coloured pencils.

Reflection

Ask, 'I wonder what is special about your tent? I wonder how you could improve your tent?'

Workshop 1B (Curriculum link: Art)

Learning intention

Children learn about the nomadic journey of Abraham and Sarah, reflecting on how Abraham worshipped God as he travelled, and how people worship now.

Engagement

Read Genesis 12:1–9 and generate questions about why Abram made altars. Ask, 'I wonder what an altar is? I wonder why Abram made altars? I wonder how Abram felt when he worshipped at his altars? I wonder how an altar could be made?'

Show pictures of uncovered altars (outside as well as in churches, made of stone and wood) and cairns and Andy Goldsworthy's interpretation of the idea (see *Stone* by Andy Goldsworthy, Thames & Hudson, 2011).

Response

Either make a clay altar using the slab technique or make an altar from stones or pebbles, inspired by Andy Goldsworthy.

Reflection

Considering the pictures and altars made by the children, ask, 'I wonder which altar design you are drawn to? If you were designing an altar for worship, I wonder which design you would choose?'

Workshop 1C (Curriculum link: Art)

Learning intention

Children are introduced to the idea of covenant or promise and start to reflect on their own place in community across time.

Engagement

Read Genesis 15:1–6 and, with music playing, show pictures from outer space, such as the Milky Way.

Read the following Bible verses.

The Lord created the stars and put them in place.
He turns darkness to dawn and daylight to darkness;
he scoops up the ocean and empties it on the earth
(Amos 5:8).

God alone stretched out the sky, stepped on the sea, and set the stars in place—the Great Bear and Orion (Job 9:8–9).

Response

Respond to the idea of the covenant, talking about generations of people being like 'stars in the sky'. Represent the myriad stars through printing or silk painting or batik.

Invite the children to generate questions about the themes. They might raise questions about the pictures of stars, the covenant between God and Abraham, the idea that Abraham was invited by God to think of all the future generations by looking at the stars in the sky, or the way they themselves feel about the stars or about being part of a long history or family of people. Questions could be displayed on sticky notes or paper stars.

Reflection

Ask, 'I wonder what is special about stars? I wonder if we've captured something of this specialness?'

As an alternative or additional activity, represent the journey through the desert using the Godly Play method of storytelling. Think about the specks of dust mentioned by God in Genesis 13:14–18. Look at sand, feel it, explore its qualities, show sand-filled bottles with layers of coloured sand, then make your own sand pictures or sand-filled bottles.

Workshop 1D
(Curriculum link: Drama and Dance)

Learning intention

Interpret the story and meaning of Abraham and Sarah's journey, through drama or dance.

Engagement

Recap the story from Genesis 12:1–9 and 13:1–18. Think back to the Godly Play story at the beginning of the day (if you presented the story in this way).

Response

Either act out the story from an unusual character's point of view, such as the camel's (there is an example in *Worship Interactive* by Michael Forster, Kevin Mayhew, 2002) or choreograph a dance about going on a journey —the dangers you might meet, resting, marking the way, and arriving. Depending on the age group, the children could be involved in the choreography.

Reflection

Discuss together your reflection on the performances, using three stars and a wish.

Workshop 2: Be communicative

Workshop 2A
(Curriculum link: Thinking and questioning)

Learning intention

Children raise questions about the story and think about its significance today for Christians and themselves.

Engagement

Recall the Godly Play or *More Bible Storybags* version of the story from the introductory session (if you used it) and display information from different charities, such as Christian Aid or CAFOD. Think about ways in which we can support charities.

Response

Using PMI, think about Abraham and Sarah's decision to obey God, and about our response to charitable organisations' requests to ask us to help others. Divide the class into groups of four. Allow five minutes for each part.

- P (Plus): What are the good points about Abraham and Sarah doing as God asks? Feed back your response to the class.
- M (Minus): What are the minus points about Abraham and Sarah doing as God asks? Feed back your response to the class.
- I (Interesting): What are the interesting points about Abraham and Sarah doing as God asks? Feed back your response to the class.

Repeat the process for your response to requests from charities such as Christian Aid to help others who are experiencing famine, drought, or refugee status.

Reflection

Ask, 'I wonder how thinking about Abraham and Sarah's story helps us to make decisions about helping other people?'

Workshop 2B
(Curriculum link: PE, PSHE)

Learning intention

Children explore what it means to trust someone and relate their findings to the story of Abraham's trust in God.

Engagement

Generate ideas about the following questions: 'I wonder what it is like to trust someone? I wonder who you trust? I wonder what it might be like for believers to trust God? I wonder how Abraham trusted God?'

Response

Set out an obstacle course using PE equipment, or design a course around the school grounds. Explain that the children will take it in turns to be the leader or blindfolded 'truster' and go round the course. Ask the children to be aware of their feelings when they are in role, as they will be sharing them afterwards.

Reflection

Ask, 'I wonder what it felt like to be the leader? I wonder what it felt like to be blindfolded?'

Explore together how the ideas about Abraham and his family being on an unknown journey but trusting God to guide and protect them can be related to modern-day life.

Workshop 2C (Curriculum link: PSHE, Citizenship, Literacy)

Learning intention

Children look at biblical poetry and consider themes of anticipation, thankfulness, support and protection.

Engagement

Read Psalm 67 and Psalm 121. Explain that Jewish people used these psalms when arriving at or departing from the temple at festival times. Generate questions and ideas about the statement, 'I wonder why Jewish people used these psalms?'

Response

The children write their own poem or psalm about protection in the same style. Then, in groups, they write a psalm that could be used in the same way for Christians as they arrive at church, or in school as children arrive at collective worship.

Reflection

Read the famous 'Footprints in the sand' poem. How does this demonstrate the same principles? Ask, 'I wonder what it would feel like to have God's protection? I wonder who you turn to for support?'

Workshop 2D (Curriculum link: PSHE)

Learning intention

Children explore how we deal with worries, or what it is like to be a refugee or new arrival.

Engagement

Watch U2's 'Walk on' video or listen to the track (from *All That You Can't Leave Behind*). Look at stories about refugees (see web links, page 94).

Response

Generate questions and produce a mind map of ideas, including the questions, 'I wonder who you turn to for support? I wonder how you'd deal with the situation? I wonder what it's like to be a refugee or new arrival? I wonder if you have ever felt like that?'

Alternatively, write questions on one-colour sticky notes, then generate possible answers and write them on different-coloured sticky notes.

Reflection

Look at each other's mind maps or the board full of questions and possible answers.

Workshop 2E (Curriculum link: Literacy)

Learning intention

Children learn about prayer, reflecting particularly upon evening prayer, and write their own prayer.

Engagement

Lead the following guided visualisation, pausing where the ellipses are shown.

Close your eyes… Imagine you are putting on your coat and going out through the door on a dark and starry night… Find somewhere comfortable to sit or lie down. Look up at the sky… See how many stars there are… Look to see if you can find any patterns of stars; perhaps you know Orion with his belt of stars in a row… I wonder which is the brightest star…? I wonder which star is the furthest away…? I wonder how it makes you feel, looking up at all those stars…? Now imagine you are standing up and walking back into the house… Put your hands over your eyes… Notice the sounds around you… With your hands still over your eyes, open your eyes.

Response

Write prayers for the night time, or blessings. Read examples from *Goodnight Prayers* by Sophie Piper. Look at the service of Compline, which is a traditional night service from, for example, the Northumbria community (see web link, page 94).

Generate ideas and questions about night prayers. Ask, 'I wonder what makes a good goodnight prayer or blessing?'

Children can write their own poem or psalm about protection or the wonder of a starry sky. You could provide a framework or decorated paper.

Reflection

Share what the children have written. If time is short, share lines or phrases.

Workshop 2F (Curriculum link: Literacy, PSHE, SMSC)

Learning intention

Children explore the idea that people don't just have physical needs; there are spiritual, emotional and moral aspects to being human (values and commitments).

Engagement

Play the game 'I went on a journey and in my suitcase I took…'

Response

Remind children of the beginning of the Godly Play story when Abraham set off on his journey with all his family. What did he need? Encourage the children to think of needs other than physical objects, such as courage, hope, faith, and so on.

Give each group a small suitcase or outline of a suitcase and ask them to put everything Abraham would need in a suitcase (write down the items or draw pictures or symbols). Starting with the most important things, children should take it in turns to choose something, justify their choice, and then group the items into 'agree' or 'disagree'.

As an extension activity, ask children to think about what they would leave out if they had to discard one thing they have chosen. For example, is it better to have courage or faith? Older or more able children could look at whether the choice would be the same for the story if they were Jewish, Christian or Islamic.

Reflection

Share and compare what everyone put in Abraham's suitcase and why.

Workshop 2G (Curriculum link: Literacy, Thinking and questioning)

Learning intention

Using their imaginations, children reflect on how Abraham might have shared his religious experience with Sarai and how she might have responded.

Engagement

Read Genesis 17:15–18. Imagine that Abraham arrives back at the house and tells Sarah what God told him when he went out to pray. Generate questions that Sarah might have asked, that Abraham might have asked, or your own questions. Write the questions on a flipchart or whiteboard.

Response

In pairs, write a conversation between Abraham and Sarah when he returned and told her what had happened. Consider having a writing frame or scribes for young or less able children.

Reflection

Share one or two of the conversations.

'My Journey' reflection

Complete the 'My Journey' reflection book during this session or during the next school day.

On a small piece of paper, draw a picture or symbol to illustrate Abraham and Sarah's journey and write the date next to it. Cut this out and stick it on to the timeline in the 'My Journey' book.

Generate an open or interesting question about the story and write it in the reflection book. Alternatively, children could answer the question, 'I wonder what the key moment of the story is and why?' and write the answer in their reflection book.

Younger children could draw the key moment. Use scribes if necessary. It is important that a copy of the child's thoughts is included in the book in order for them to look back on their journey as they progress through the school.

Children should share their thoughts with a response partner.

Workshop 3: Be knowledgeable

Workshop 3A (Curriculum link: Science, Geography)

Learning intention

In order to understand better what it was like on the journey, children find out about climate and environment in the parts of the world that Abraham travelled through.

Engagement

Show photos from all the areas that Abraham travelled through. Ask, 'I wonder what it would be like to live or travel through each of these places? I wonder what kind of information you would need to find out? I wonder where you could find it?'

Response

Provide climate information, maps, photos of terrain, RE books about life and times in the Bible (see page 11, suitable websites, and so on). In groups, investigate what it would be like to live in each of the different environments, and think about what this information would mean for Abram and his family at each stage of the journey—Babylon delta, desert, Canaan (including drought times) and Egypt.

Reflection

Share what you have found out.

Workshop 3B (Curriculum link: Science)

Learning intention

Children explore the interconnectedness of everything on a fundamental level, relating this to the story of Abraham and Sarah and how we are interconnected across time.

Engagement

Show a picture of the universe and a picture of a molecule of an element such as carbon. Everything—human beings, planets and the earth—is made out of the same building blocks (the elements). Everything is interconnected because of its chemical composition.

Recap the part of the story where God asks Abraham to look at the stars and think about all the generations of people to come (Genesis 15:1–6). We are all made of the chemical elements in stardust.

Response

Set the children the task of discovering what the body is made of.

99 per cent of the mass of the human body is made up of just six elements: oxygen, carbon, hydrogen, nitrogen, calcium and phosphorus. Most of the human body is made up of water, H_2O, with cells consisting of 65–90 per cent water by weight. Therefore, it isn't surprising that most of a human body's mass is oxygen (65 per cent) and hydrogen (10 per cent). Carbon, the basic unit for organic molecules, comes in second largest at 18 per cent, ahead of the other three elements.

Carbon is unique among the elements in the vast number and variety of compounds it can form. With hydrogen, oxygen, nitrogen and other elements, it forms a very large number of compounds, carbon atom often being linked to carbon atom. There are over ten million known carbon compounds, many thousands of which are vital to organic and life processes. Without carbon, life on earth would not be possible.

Use K-Nex, Magnetix, cocktail sticks and raisins, dried fruit or something similar to build models of carbon molecules such as diamond or graphite (see web link, page 94).

Reflection

Ask, 'I wonder what it feels like to know that everything is made of the same stuff? I wonder if a combination of elements is all that we are?'

Look at the children's models of carbon molecules. Ask, 'I wonder what it feels like to know that we are all interconnected across time, like all the generations since Abraham, or across society as interdependent and fellow citizens of earth?'

Workshop 3C (Curriculum link: Maths)

Learning intention

Children explore the puzzle of how we might count the stars in the sky and relate this to the story of Abraham and Sarah, considering how something ordinary was used to give a significant message.

Engagement

Show a picture of millions of stars on a whiteboard. Read Genesis 15:1–6, where God tells Abraham that he will have as many children as there are stars in the sky. Generate questions about how many stars there are and write the questions around the picture.

Response

In pairs, work out a method for counting the stars (see, for example, the great worldwide star count—web link on page 94). Alternatively, as individuals, make mathematical star patterns by drawing random dots on a piece of paper and then linking them with lines, using a ruler, or make origami stars from different-sized squares of paper (see web link for printed origami instructions).

Reflection

God asked Abraham to look at the stars so that he could explain something to him. Ask, 'I wonder if you have ever had a flash of inspiration when looking at something very familiar?'

Workshop 3D (Curriculum link: History)

Learning intention

Children explore what it means to belong to a family and think about how Christians might feel about belonging to the Christian family.

Engagement

Read about Jesus' family tree (Matthew 1:1–17) and look at other family trees. Look at a family history website or a clip from the BBC programme *Who Do You Think You Are?* (web links, page 94).

Ask children to bring in information about their own family trees. (Where this information is not available or would prove to include sensitive details, please supply a family tree that children can use instead.) Provide a writing frame of a family tree to fill in for younger or less able children.

Reflection

Ask, 'What does it feel like to belong to a family? Does a family tree help you think about who you are? I wonder what Christians understand about being part of the Christian family? I wonder if it is just the physical that connects us as a family?'

Workshop 3E (Curriculum link: History, Geography, DT)

Learning intention

Children learn about nomadic lifestyles today and make links to the story of Abraham and Sarah's journey.

Engagement

Explore descriptions of nomadic life and shelters and find first-hand accounts. Find information, books and pictures showing some of the following:

- Native Americans (tepees, longhouses, lodges, adobes and wigwams)
- Traveller community (caravans, both traditional and modern)
- Bedouin (tents)
- Mongolian (yurts)
- Canal (barges)

Choose one nomadic lifestyle and look at the homes that are used. Research and collect evidence about the following for your nomadic home:

- How are they made?
- How are they made suitable for use in different climates?
- How are they packed up and transported for relocating?

Ask, 'I wonder how the people who live in them make them feel like home? I wonder what you would like or not like about living in this type of home?'

Reflection

Ask, 'I wonder what we can learn from people who live a nomadic lifestyle now, or from Abraham and Sarah's journey, about what it is like to live with fewer belongings?'

Whole-school worship

Preparation

Bring the children's artwork together and display as much as possible. As a focal point, use an IWB to show an image that represents the start of a journey. Display a suitcase with props or large labels to show what we might take on our journey in life. For example:

- Protection: sun cream, an umbrella, a raincoat
- Sustenance: picnic food or some water

- Rest and play: a comic, a book, a pillow, a game
- Knowledge: maps and guide books

Ask, 'I wonder what other things you have thought about today that you would need for life's journey?' (for example, faith, courage, trust, hope, consideration, kindness, generosity, wisdom and so on).

Celebrate the day and share what the groups or classes have done, perhaps including a dance or drama performance from one of the workshops.

Reading

Read a poem written by the children, based on Psalm 67 or Psalm 121.

Prayers

Select from *The Lion Book of 1000 Prayers for Children* (pages 421–431), including a prayer based on the story of Abraham and other stories in the Bible.

Blessing

Read a goodnight blessing written by the children.

Suggested songs

The journey of life (*Complete Come and Praise*)
Who would true valour see
One more step
As we go now (Fischy Music, 2002)
May you find peace (Fischy Music, 2006)
Going on a journey (Fischy Music, 2004)
Lord, for the years
Father Abraham (actions can be found on the internet)

Unit 3 extension material

Workshop for Foundation Stage

Engagement

Explore the wondering questions for the story as suggested in *Godly Play Volume 2* or *More Bible Storybags*.

Response

- Using a sand tray, provide a city of bricks, tents, stones for altars and model people, so that the children can retell the story for themselves.
- Make a drawing or painting of families.
- Make a 'caravan' train and go on a journey around the playground. Imagine what it's like to stop and pitch your tent, go to sleep under the stars, miss your friends and family, make new friends, explore new environments and so on.
- Play 'I went on a journey and in my suitcase I took…'
- Show examples of nomadic living from *Rosie and Jim* (see www.rosieandjim.tv), Native Americans and so on. Make a tent or shelter and play in it.
- Sing 'Father Abraham had many sons' (actions can be found on the internet)

Story

Suitable story books include the following.

- *Abraham's Search for God* (Jacqueline Jules (Kar-Ben, 2007)
- *Pip and the Edge of Heaven*, Elizabeth Liddle (Lion Hudson, 2003)
- *The Gruffalo*, Julia Donaldson (Macmillan, 1999)
- *Percy the Park Keeper*, Nick Butterworth (HarperCollins, 2005)
- *Going on a Bear Hunt*, Michael Rosen and Helen Oxenbury (Walker Books, 1992)
- *Rosie's Walk*, Pat Hutchins (Red Fox, 2010)

Class collective worship

Give children the opportunity to revisit the story, generate questions and ideas from the journey day and add thoughts, questions or responses to their journal.

Reflection

Show the children a jar filled with 100 marbles, glass nuggets or stars and ask them to guess how many there are. Ask, 'If there are 100 here, can you imagine what thousands would look like?'

Explain that the way Abraham and Sarah trusted God was so important that it was mentioned in the New Testament 2000 years later to teach people about following and trusting God. Read Hebrews 11:1–3 and 8–12. Explain that Abraham and Sarah's faith took them on a journey and supported them on that journey. God promised that they would have as many descendants as there are stars in the sky. Even though this seemed impossible, Sarah and Abraham still trusted God.

Show a picture of thousands of stars on the whiteboard and pour out a cupful of sand, noting that there are thousands of grains. Even though there are now thousands, millions and even billions of people in the world, the Bible teaches that each person is known to God by name. Read Isaiah 43:1 ('Don't be afraid. I have rescued you. I have called you by name; now you belong to me').

Response

Put every child's name into a sack or basket. Each child draws out the name of another child in the class. Ask children to write that name on a star and add something special about that person.

Reflection

Create a class star display. How does it feel to be on the star board or to write a star for someone else?

Looking back on the journey

Plan a time of reflection for staff, governors and church visitors. Share some of the experiences from the school journey day, or any follow-up work that has occurred within school or church.

Read Genesis 17:5 and 15. Talk about how Abraham and Sarah thought that their lives together would follow one pattern, but God had a much bigger vision for their lives. Through faith, Abraham and Sarah were able to fulfil God's purposes for themselves and to influence future generations, history and faith. The change of their names is symbolic of the transformation that took place in their lives and a public acknowledgement of their calling.

Response

Ask, 'Looking back, I wonder where your plans have been changed? I wonder what good purposes might come out of a change of direction?'

Ask, 'Looking ahead, I wonder what you see planned? I wonder what you feel called to do? Are these two things the same?'

Look at a photograph of an untrodden snow-covered path and think about the direction that you might take. Imagine your footprints in the snow. Difficult times can feel like an uphill struggle. Ask, 'I wonder where you will draw strength from for the journey?'

Conclude the reflection with a time of silence or quiet music followed by the blessing below.

Blessing

May God shield you on every step. May Christ aid you on every path. May Spirit fill you on every slope, on hill and on plain.

CARMINA GADELICA

Unit 3 church-based activity day

This can be a full day, half day or after-school club session.

Setting the scene

As a focal point, set out some bread, a tent, some 'desert' sand, a suitcase, a blank map, and a copy of Rublev's icon of the Trinity (available on the internet). If you have media facilities, show pictures of the places that Abraham travelled to, accompanied by music. Display a Bible timeline such as *The Big Bible Storybook Timeline*.

Read Genesis 18:1–15 and Hebrews 11:1–3 and 8–12. Show Rublev's icon and explain that you are going to explore the themes of hospitality in the story.

Suggested activities

- Look at pictures of Rublev's icon and other versions showing Abraham and Sarah as well as the three visitors. Explain what an icon is. Talk about what you think the icon shows. Explain that the figures are the three visitors in the story—traditionally three angels. Notice how the fourth place, at the open side of the table, is empty. Ask, 'I wonder why it is empty?' Explain that, traditionally, people think it is making room for us to come in to the picture. Make individual or group welcoming icons.
- In Genesis 18:1–7, Abraham uses hospitality as an opportunity to extend blessing. Think about how people are welcomed into church in a regular service or a special service, such as a toddler service, a seasonal celebration or a wedding. What could be done differently? Create a 'code of welcome' for different occasions. You might like to make a design for the entrance or create badges for people whose job it is to welcome others into church. Think about the end of the service. In what ways are people made to feel at home as they leave the church?
- Make bread either in a bread machine or by hand, using a recipe for unleavened bread, a bread mix or soda bread, which is quick and easy. You could share bread at the meal later.
- Make decorated name tags and hang them on a plan of a church family tree. You could decorate the plan with patterns or images of things that are important to the church. Talk about how Christians believe that we are all part of the family of God.
- Bedouin hospitality still follows the law of the desert, which requires that if a stranger appears at your tent, you must welcome them and share your food, drink and shelter, just as Abraham did. In the heat of the desert, it is a matter of human survival. You welcome others and they welcome you in return. There are many biblical examples of hospitality and care by God and God's people, such as God's provision of manna and quails in the desert (Exodus 16:1–36), Moses living with Jethro (or Reuel), the priest of Midian (Exodus 2:16–22), and Jesus' teaching about hospitality (Matthew 25:35–36). Make a PowerPoint presentation or collage with images for each of the lines in Matthew 25:35–36.
- Look at pictures of the Durham Cathedral sanctuary door knocker (available on the internet). Think about refugees, and talk about initiatives in your area, such as soup kitchens and charities that support refugees or others who are finding life difficult, such as homeless people. Think about your next harvest festival and who you could help.
- Think about prayers that Abraham might have said at the altars he made in the different places he visited. Look around the room or church building (you could use photographs if it is not possible to go into the church). Write prayers to say at different places around the room or church.

Make or bring and share food together, including the bread if you made some earlier. Say or sing a grace and choose children, young people and adults to bring an icon, bread, a welcome notice and a cross to the front. Ask them to talk about what each item signifies or symbolises in terms of the hospitality that we offer at home or in school, or that Christians might offer in church.

Worship

Conclude with one or more versions of a welcome prayer written during the activities.

Sing 'Father Abraham had many sons'.

UNIT 4

Ruth's journey

Bible focus

Ruth 1—4
Leviticus 19:9; 23:22
Deuteronomy 24:19–21
Matthew 1:1–17

Programme for the day

9.00–9.30am	Whole-school introduction to the day
9.30–10.35am	Workshops 1 and 2 (combined)
10.35–10.55am	Break
10.55–12.00	Workshops 1 and 2 (continued)
12.00–1.00pm	Lunch
1.00–1.15pm (or next day)	'My Journey' reflection
1.15–2.20pm	Workshop 3
2.20–2.30pm	Break
2.30–3.00pm	Whole-school worship

Preparation

Plan a time of reflection on the theme for the staff, governors and church visitors. Read the story of Ruth from a story Bible, such as *The Book of Books* by Trevor Dennis (Lion Hudson, 2009) or a similar shortened version. Consider the main themes of the story—setting out into the unknown, standing beside someone through thick and thin, being a stranger in a new place, acceptance, kindness, God's knowledge of Ruth's potential, Ruth's faith journey, and so on.

Ask, 'I wonder if you can relate this to your own life or today's society? I wonder what we can learn from Ruth's story?'

Think about what it means to offer someone else a welcome. Ask, 'I wonder what it is like to be a stranger... to be standing beside someone when it would be easier to walk away... to trust others and to trust God when things seem impossible?'

Reflection

Hold a grain of wheat or corn and think about the potential of your community, the school, the church and the people around. Conclude the reflection with a time of silence or quiet music.

Prayer

Lord, we pray that we will encourage one another as we prepare for the weeks ahead in school, church and community. We ask that you will equip us to be both welcoming and trusting and always ready to see potential in one another and situations. Amen

Whole-school introduction to the day

Set up a focal point with some ripe wheat and pictures of harvest. On an IWB, show *Triptych, 2000* by Roger Wagner (see web link, page 94).

To explore the painting, ask, 'I wonder what this painting might be about? I wonder who the people are in the painting? I wonder why it is in three sections?'

Discuss each question in pairs, then share some responses.

Read the story of Ruth from a children's Bible such as *The Lion Storyteller Bible*, *More Bible Storybags* or *Godly Play Volume 6*.

Sing one of the following songs.

- We thank you, God, for all that you have given us (Out of the Ark)
- When I needed a neighbour
- Would you walk by on the other side? (*Complete Come and Praise*, BBC Active, 1990)
- Make me a channel of your peace

Explain that the children will come back at the end of the day and share what they have discovered about the story of Ruth.

Prayer

For harvest around the world, O God, we thank you.
For the people who pick the crops, O God,
we thank you.
For the people who deliver our food and work in the shops, O God, we thank you.
For the food we share together and share with others, O God, we thank you.
For all the things we will learn together and share together this day, O God, we thank you. Amen

BARBARA MEARDON

Use the wheat, a copy of the triptych and questions to make a reflection corner in school or church. (For ideas, see the *Pause for Reflection* pack.)

Workshops 1 and 2 (combined): Be creative and communicative

Curriculum link: Art, Speaking and listening, Thinking and questioning

All groups or classes will create their own painting, or a section of a painting of their choice, to make a class triptych or a painting to represent one part of the story only. The workshops will last all morning to allow time to explore the ideas and create a finished piece of work.

Learning intention

Children look at how artists have represented the story of Ruth. Consider the most important aspects of the story, the meaning of the story for Christians and the meaning for themselves. They will then represent their ideas using art.

Engagement

Show a painting of the story from the selection below.

- *Triptych, 2000* by Roger Wagner
- Triptych *The Story of Ruth* by Thomas Matthews Rooke (1875)
- *Ruth in the Fields* by Merle Hughes
- *Ruth in Boaz's Field* (National Gallery) by Julius Schnorr von Carolsfeld (1828)
- *Ruth and Naomi* by He Qi

For more images and background information, see web links on page 94.

Talk about how the artists have represented the themes and ideas in the story by asking the following questions.

- I wonder how the artist who made the triptych shows meaning through the techniques he uses, such as brushstrokes, colour, composition? How does this convey key meanings and themes of the story of Ruth?
- I wonder how the painting helps you understand the story of Ruth?
- I wonder how the part of the story your group is focusing on is depicted in the picture?

Response

Recreate a section or aspect of the painting or make a class triptych using any of the following suggestions.

- Make seed pictures.
- Use junk or litter (gleaned).
- Use collage materials.
- Make a 3D representation such as paper sculpture or clay.
- Put together photographs or moving images, using PhotoStory or similar to recreate the story.
- Modernise the picture by superimposing changes to the scene.
- Create a still-life painting or drawing of corn.
- Use pastels to explore one section of the painting.
- Make a whole picture from individual tiles of a section of the painting put together to make the whole.
- Make a tissue picture overdrawn with pen, inspired by Raoul Dufy.

Talk about the themes and ideas from the story, what meaning they might have for Christians and what meanings they might have for the children themselves. Make a note of questions raised, comments and feelings expressed by the children.

Reflection

Share responses as a whole group or class and, if desired, display responses on a board. (With younger children, use a scribe.)

'My Journey' reflection

Complete the 'My Journey' reflection book during this session or during the next school day. On a small piece of paper, draw a picture or symbol to illustrate Ruth's journey and write the date next to it. Cut this out and stick it on to the timeline in the 'My Journey' book.

Generate an open or interesting question about the story and write it in the reflection book. Alternatively, in their books, ask the children to respond to the question, 'What is the key moment of the story and why does it matter?'

Younger children could draw the key moment. Use scribes if necessary (it is important that a copy of the child's thoughts is included in the book in order for them to see their journey).

Children should share their thoughts with a response partner.

Workshop 3: Be communicative and be knowledgeable

Workshop 3A (Curriculum link: Thinking and questioning, PSHE)

Learning intention

Children think about their own experiences of being or feeling like an outsider. They will then explore the ways in which Ruth was an outsider. What happened that meant Ruth no longer felt like an outsider? What has helped us not to feel like an outsider? How could we help someone who feels like an outsider?

Engagement

Show *Triptych, 2000* again and talk about Ruth being an outsider. Generate questions about what this might have been like for Ruth and make a list of the 'feeling' words that the children use. Ask, 'I wonder how we can know what it feels like to be an outsider? I wonder how we would feel as an outsider? I wonder who might feel like an outsider in today's society and why? I wonder if there are times when someone might feel like an outsider in our school?'

Response

Find suitable pictures of people who might feel like outsiders, such as street children, refugees, homeless people and disabled people, and a picture to represent all of us (because anyone can feel like an outsider). In pairs, explore what it is like to be an outsider nowadays; look at one of the pictures representing someone who might feel like an outsider and generate questions you'd like to ask of the person, the photographer and society as a whole. Share your ideas about your photograph with another pair: what is similar or different about your photos and ideas?

Reflection

Ask, 'I wonder if there are similarities in all these photos and ideas?' Look at the 'feeling' words generated earlier. Ask, 'I wonder what we could do to stop someone feeling like an outsider?'

Workshop 3B (Curriculum link: Dance, Art)

Learning intention

Explore how the artist shows meaning through the body postures of the people in the triptych. Using body movements, explore the key meanings and themes of the story.

Engagement

Look at the body postures that the artist has painted in the triptych.

Response

Recreate the postures and use them to tell the story of the three pictures. Alternatively, explore the themes of plenty, struggle, sharing, supporting and celebrating through a sequence of movement or dance.

Reflection

Using three stars and a wish, share responses on the quality of the movement or dance and how effectively the children have communicated their ideas.

Workshop 3C (Curriculum link: Literacy)

Learning intention

Reflect on the story of Ruth and the children's own experiences, and discuss how people are made to feel welcome.

Engagement

Talk about the idea of hospitality. Explain that, in Celtic Christianity in particular, there is the idea of welcoming your neighbour as you would welcome Jesus. Look at examples of welcome packs, cards or leaflets and discuss how they would help people to feel welcome. See, for example, the web links on page 95.

Response

Make a welcome book for new children arriving at your school. Discuss what you would need to include. How could language, photographs or pictures be used to convey welcome?

Reflection

Ask, 'I wonder if a book would be enough to make people feel welcome? I wonder what else we might need to do to make people feel welcome?'

Workshop 3D (Curriculum link: Literacy)

Learning intention

Children reflect on the story of Ruth and identify the key elements and meanings of the story and what they might mean for them.

Engagement

Tell the story using *Godly Play Volume 6, More Bible Storybags* or Bible Society's 'Testament: Bible in Animation' DVD: *Ruth* (see web link, page 95). Use the questions included in *Godly Play* or *More Bible Storybags*. Alternatively, think about the various people in the painting or on the DVD. Consider them as witnesses of the story, discussing their different experiences and viewpoints.

Response

In groups, use hot-seating as a way to question or interview the characters. With the information gathered, create a newspaper report or write ideas on laminated thinking, speech and feeling bubbles for that character. (With younger children, use a scribe to record ideas.)

Reflection

Share some of the responses.

Workshop 3E (Curriculum link: Literacy)

Learning intention

Children explore the theme of harvest from the story of Ruth.

Engagement

Read the poem 'Seeds' from *Seed Poems* by John Foster (OUP, 1991). Ruth was gleaning at harvest time, collecting the grain that had been left behind. (For information about gleaning, see the web link on page 95.) The custom of gleaning goes back to the early agricultural laws of the Hebrews (see Leviticus 19:9; 23:22; Deuteronomy 24:19–21).

Seeds are important sources of food and have the potential to grow into new plants. Think about and discuss the potential that God saw in Ruth, the good deeds that both Boaz and Ruth did, and the potential we have to do good.

Response

Using seeds and growth as a metaphor, write a poem about our potential to grow personally and to do good and make a difference.

Reflection

Share some golden lines or whole poems with the class.

Workshop 3F (Curriculum link: History, Geography, ICT)

Learning intention

In order to understand the story of Ruth, children will look at ancient farming techniques.

Engagement

The story is set in Israel, and Roger Wagner's *Triptych, 2000* is a view of a cornfield. Ask, 'I wonder what you can tell about farming at that time from the painting?'

Response

Research farming in ancient Israel. See www.Bible-archaeology.info/work.htm; *The Lion Encyclopedia of the Bible, Journey through Bible Lands* or *Life in Bible Times* (see page 11).

Reflection

Read the story of Ruth, pausing each time you come to a farming term and asking the children to explain the process. Ask, 'I wonder if you understand the story better now that we have found out more about life in Bible times?'

Workshop 3G (Curriculum link: Citizenship)

Learning intention

Children look at how people provided for those in need at the time of Ruth and explore how we do the same now.

Engagement

Look at the painting made in the morning workshop and talk about how Boaz allowed poorer people to pick grain from the edges of the field. Ask, 'I wonder why he did this?'

Explain that the custom of gleaning goes back to the early agricultural laws of the Hebrews (see Leviticus 19:9; 23:22; Deuteronomy 24:19–21). Ruth was collecting the grain that had been left behind.

Response

Using PMI, evaluate the questions 'Is it good to leave grain at the sides of the field for poor people?' and 'Should we provide for the needy people in our society?'

Reflection

Ask, 'I wonder what are the similarities and differences between what society did then and what we do now? I wonder what we can learn from the story of Ruth about how we look after people? I wonder if you understand the story better now that we have found out more about life in Bible times?'

Workshop 3H (Curriculum link: Maths, Geography)

Learning intention

Children look at the route and terrain encountered by Ruth on her journey, in order to understand the story better and think about how long it would have taken.

Engagement

Look at the route of Ruth and Naomi's journey. See, for example, *Nelson's Complete Book of Bible Maps and Charts* (Thomas Nelson, 2002) or the web link on page 95. Generate questions that you would need answers to, in order to understand what the journey was like for Ruth and Naomi, such as 'I wonder how people travelled?', 'I wonder how far it is?', 'I wonder where they started and finished their journey?' and so on.

Response

In groups, find out about the route and terrain encountered by Ruth and Naomi on their journey, and how people travelled at that time. See, for example, *The Lion Encyclopedia of the Bible*, *Journey through Bible Lands* or *Life in Bible Times* (see page 11). Find a way to present the information you have found out to the class. For example, make a poster, leaflet, drama, interview, documentary or PowerPoint presentation.

Reflection

Share responses. Ask, 'I wonder if you understand the story better now that we have found out more about life in Bible times?'

Workshop 3I (Curriculum link: History)

Learning intention

In order to understand the story of Ruth, children look at homes and family life in ancient Israel.

Engagement

Explore homes and family life at the time of Ruth. Look at who was living in the family at the beginning of the story. Ask, 'I wonder what we can know about how families lived at the time of Ruth from the story? I wonder how families then were different from our families now?' Consider issues such as the nuclear family, and so on.

Response

In groups, research one aspect of family life, such as homes, clothing and jewellery, marriage customs, food and cooking. See *The Lion Encyclopedia of the Bible*, *Journey through Bible Lands* or *Life in Bible Times* (see page 11), or the web links on page 95.

In the same groups, make a mind map of what the children have found out. Using an envoying technique, share what you have found out. Ask children to discuss their own ideas or complete their own piece of research. Each group then sends an 'envoy' to share their ideas or information with another group. The envoy may be chosen by the group, preselected and notified by the teacher, or selected by the teacher but only notified immediately before being sent (see web link, page 95). Each group adds extra information, brought by the envoys from other groups, to their mind map.

Reflection

Ask, 'I wonder if you understand the story better now that we have found out more about life in Bible times?'

Whole-school worship

Preparation

At lunch time and at the end of the day, ask for volunteers to display artwork in the worship area.

Explain that God walked beside Ruth into the

unknown, and Ruth trusted Naomi and said, 'Your God will be my God.' She trusted that all would be well. Draw large individual letters for the word 'harvest' and use them to spell out 'have', 'rest', 'vast', 'eat', 'heat', 'starve' and 'save'. Talk about how each of these words applies to the day. End with the word 'share', and ask children from each class to share poems, dance, music, thoughts, experiences and feelings about what they have done during the day.

Reflection

Hold a hazelnut in your hand and explain that Julian of Norwich was a holy woman who lived in the Middle Ages. An inspiring story about her tells how she felt that God asked her to hold a small hazelnut in her hand. A hazelnut is a seed full of potential, just like the grains of wheat that Ruth gleaned at the harvest. Julian said, 'In this little thing I saw that God made it, God loves it and God keeps it.' She believed that in the same way as God made, loves and cares for all of creation, including the hazelnut, he also cares for us. Reflect for a moment on how Christians believe that God made us, loves us and keeps us. (For a biography of Julian, see the web link on page 95.)

Prayer

Lord, we do not know what lies ahead
or where we are to go.
We pray for a straight road, smooth travelling,
a safe arrival.
We pray that we will know that you are with us
as we journey.
Grant us hope and courage as we travel,
and inspiring moments along the way. Amen

BARBARA MEARDON

Suggested songs

He's got the whole world in his hands (*Complete Come and Praise*)
God is love, his the care

Blessing

A well-known saying from Julian of Norwich is that 'All will be well and all manner of things will be well.' We ask that God will bless each one of us and that all will be well. Amen

Unit 4 extension material

Workshop for Foundation Stage

Engagement

Tell the story using *Godly Play Volume 6, More Bible Storybags* or the 'Testament: Bible in Animation' DVD: *Ruth*.

Response

Use a sand tray to re-enact the story with figures, or dress up and tell the story. Explore ways to grind corn, make a seed picture or talk about caring for other people.

Suitable story books

- *Seed Poems*, John Foster (OUP, 1991)
- *Giraffes Can't Dance*, Giles Andreae (Orchard Books, 2007)
- *Little Beaver and the Echo*, Amy MacDonald (Walker, 1993)
- *Angelina's Dance of Friendship*, Helen Craig (American Girl, 2004)
- *I Want a Friend*, Tony Ross (Andersen, 2005)

Class collective worship

Remind the children of the story and then give each child a seed or grain of corn. Ask, 'I wonder what it has to have to make it grow? If we are full of potential like a seed, I wonder what else is needed or helps us grow and fulfil our potential?' Explore possible answers, such as love, friendship, care, encouragement, praise, success, experience, and so on.

Ask, 'I wonder what potential you have?' Suggest to the children that they could write about this in their 'My Journey' reflection book. Alternatively, give children the opportunity to revisit the story, generate questions and ideas from the journey day and add thoughts, questions or responses to their journal.

Reflection

Generate thinking about times when children have been encouraged to use their gifts and when they have encouraged somebody else. Think about acts of kindness, such as the times when Ruth was kind to Naomi, and Boaz was kind to Ruth. Point out that what they did was an integral part of their faith, acted out in their lives.

Think about what a difference it could make if we all did more random acts of kindness for friends, family, classmates or people we don't know. For stories and lesson plans, see the web links on page 95. There are also books about random acts of kindness.

Give children a strip of paper that says 'random act of kindness' to take home. Explain that they should bring it back and pin it to the class board once they have acted upon it.

Prayer

Lord God, we pray that we can make a difference in your world through random acts of kindness. Amen

Looking back on the journey

Plan a time of reflection on the theme for staff, governors and church visitors. Reflect on some of the experiences from the school journey day or any follow-up work that has occurred within the school or church. Looking back over the story of Ruth, reflect on:

- What you have learned.
- What you have enjoyed.
- What you have been grateful for.
- What you have changed.
- What you have received from others.
- What you have given to others.

Think about random acts of kindness. Look at some examples and think about what a difference it could make if we all did more acts of kindness, for friends, family or strangers.

Reflect on how you might consciously look for opportunities to carry out random acts of kindness in your daily life, and follow this reflection with a time of silence or quiet music.

Prayer

Help us to see the opportunities to share your love and transform your world through acts of kindness and generosity. We ask this in your name. Amen

Unit 4 church-based activity day

This can be a full day, half day or after-school club session.

Setting the scene

Set up a focal point by showing pictures of fields of corn or people on a journey, accompanied by music. Display a Bible timeline such as *The Big Bible Storybook Timeline*.

Read the story of Ruth from a children's Bible, such as *The Barnabas Children's Bible*.

Suggested activities

- Think about Ruth moving from one country to another. Bring an inflatable or soft toy globe. Standing or sitting in a circle, take it in turns to throw and catch or roll the globe to each other. When you catch the globe, point to somewhere that you've been to or know about and pray a blessing on that place. Look at crosses from around the world, representing the worldwide church. (See *A-cross the World* by Martyn Payne and Betty Pedley or www.barnabasinchurches.org.uk/a-cross-the-world.) Provide materials and instructions to make some of the crosses.
- Remind everyone that Ruth arrived in Bethlehem as a stranger and was befriended by Naomi's relative, Boaz. Read Deuteronomy 10:18–20 and Matthew 25:35. Find out about the Birmingham Churches Together project that seeks to help, welcome and support refugees and asylum seekers. Explain about their befriending scheme (see web links, page 95).

  Read the Kids' page on the Restore website (see web link, page 95), then create a card or leaflet that would explain the role to a potential befriender or would tell a refugee about the scheme.

  Information about refugees that is suitable for children and young people is also available from The Children's Society. Look at their 'What we do' statement and the refugee section, including examples of specific programmes such as the 'Include' project in Southampton and the 'Embrace' project. They also have information about projects supporting runaways (see web link, page 95).

  See also the work of Christian Aid or CAFOD (see web links, page 95). Write some facts about refugees or generate questions about refugees and our response to them on cards or luggage labels.
- Read Matthew 25:35 and design a card, bookmark or gift box that you could give to someone new to your church (see YouTube or www.origami-fun.com for instructions). Ask, 'I wonder what sort of gift we could put in the box, or what message you would write on a card? Would you put a label on your box? I wonder what it would say?' Think of items such as chocolates, an invitation to tea, a flower, some soap, and so on.
- Look at the artwork used to inspire the school journey day and talk about the themes of the story of Ruth. Use these ideas to make an altar frontal, a banner, a stained-glass window or vestments for a minister in the church.
- Display two wooden crosses and some sticky tack. Draw round hands and feet on brightly coloured paper and cut out the shapes. Explain that the cross of hands will represent joining in friendship and the cross of feet will represent the idea that we are all travelling along on the journey together, whether or not we are friends.

  Write a prayer or draw a picture on the hand shapes and pray for help to make friends, to care for people and so on. Write a prayer or draw a picture on the foot shapes and pray for the journey through life and in different places. Stick the hand and foot shapes to the cross with sticky tack.

Make or bring and share food together and say or sing a grace.

Worship

Gather in front of the altar frontal, banner, stained-glass window or vestment that you have made and invite two people to carry the two crosses, covered in hands and feet, to the front. Read Matthew 25:35 and welcome everyone to the worship. Show some of the crosses from around the world and ask people to explain where their cross is from and what it represents. Ask people to hold up their crosses and ask God's blessing on all the people living in those places.

Sing a song from somewhere else in the world, such as 'Siyahamba', or 'Allelu-allelu-allelu-alleluia', or sing a chant from Taizé such as 'Nada de turbe' (Let nothing disturb you).

UNIT 5

Jump into a picture: Christmas

Bible focus

Matthew 1:18—2:18
Luke 2:1–20

Programme for the day

9.00–9.30am	Whole-school introduction to the day
9.30–10.35am	Workshop 1
10.35–10.55am	Break
10.55–12.00	Workshops 2 and 3 (combined)
12.00–1.00pm	Lunch
1.00–1.15pm (or next day)	'My Journey' reflection
1.15–2.20pm	Workshops 2 and 3 (continued)
2.20–2.30pm	Break
2.30–3.00pm	Whole-school worship

Preparation

Plan a time of reflection on the theme for staff, governors and church visitors. Display a picture of the nativity chosen from the following selection, all of which can be found on the internet: 'I bring you good news' by J.D. Paterson (from *Jim's Grandiose Book of Bible Pictures*); *The Nativity* by Previtali, William Bell Scott, Bernadino di Betto, Pinturicchio, or He Qi.

Ask, 'I wonder how you respond to the picture? I wonder how you feel about the journey ahead of you this year? I wonder if any of the ideas or images in the painting has anything to say about your journey?'

If desired, share ideas at this point, either as a group or in pairs. Alternatively, each person could write a thought on a star, flower or cross shape and place it around a lighted candle. Spend some time thinking quietly about where each of you is on your journey and conclude with a short silence or by listening to quiet music.

Read Matthew 1:18—2:11 and Luke 2:1–7. If there is time, read John Betjeman's poem 'Christmas' (available on the internet).

Prayer

*May the spirit of Christmas which is Peace...
the gladness of Christmas which is Hope...
and the heart of Christmas which is Love...
be ours this day and always. Amen*

Whole-school introduction to the day

Display the picture chosen from the selection above on an IWB. Play seasonal music as the children come in, such as 'Sweet Christmas Bells' from the *Sweet Bells* CD by Kate Rusby (Pure Records, 2008). Set up a focal point using a nativity scene (keep the characters separately in a box) and a manger full of hay.

Ask, 'Who is represented in the painting? I wonder what the artist has done to show who they are?' Encourage children to note a shepherd's crook or king's crown, but also to look at symbolism. For example, Mary is traditionally dressed in blue because blue paint used to be made from lapis lazuli, which was the most precious and expensive colouring.

Ask, 'I wonder what you might ask someone in the painting? I wonder what you might ask the artist about a character? I wonder how the people in the painting are feeling at this moment in the story?'

Read the nativity story either from a modern version of the Bible or from a retelling such as *The Barnabas Children's Bible*. Alternatively, choose one of the following storytelling options.

- 'The First Christmas' from the BBC learning zone (see web link on page 95).
- 'He's here!' from *Jesus Storybook* read by David Suchet (see YouTube)
- Desmond Tutu reading from the *Children of God Storybook Bible* (see YouTube)

Ask children from each class to come forward, take the characters and animals out of the box and talk about each one as they place it in the scene.

Explain that everyone will explore a different part of the story or painting today and come back at the end of the day to share what they have enjoyed. Play seasonal music as the children go out.

Use the picture, focus and questions to make a reflection corner in school or church. For ideas, see the *Pause for Reflection* pack.

Workshop 1: The nativity

Learning intention

Children explore the story and symbolism in the picture and how they are linked to the Bible story, then respond to the story and the painting.

The following areas of focus are suggested. (This will not apply if you are using vertical/family groupings.)

- Foundation Stage: Holy family
- Year 1: Children or other ordinary people
- Year 2: Mary
- Year 3: Angels
- Year 4: Shepherds
- Year 5: Wise men
- Year 6: Extend by looking at a picture of the flight into Egypt

Engagement

Display a copy of your chosen picture on an IWB. Think about how the part of the story your group is considering is depicted in the picture. Discuss and generate questions to explore. Think about connections with other parts of the Bible, such as candles or light representing Jesus as the light of the world (John 8:12). Look at the symbolism used to depict the characters or object you are studying. How does this help you understand the nativity story?

Choose one of the following activities.

- In small groups, look at other examples of the same part of the story in paintings, sculpture or stained glass. Look for similarities and differences and share findings with the whole class.
- Write individual or class poetry, such as an acrostic, where each line begins with a letter from an appropriate word ('nativity', 'Christmas', 'shepherd' and so on) or a kenning, where each line describes what you are talking about without saying what it is (for example, a shepherd may be a 'news bringer').
- Write a first-person narrative in response to the story to describe events as they happen, as well as thoughts and feelings. For example, 'If I were Mary…'

Reflection

Share responses as a whole group or class (for younger children, use adults or older children to scribe). If desired, display responses on a board.

Workshops 2 and 3 (combined): Exploring the story

Note: Choose either one workshop to cover both time slots or two different workshops.

Learning intention

Having looked at the painting of the nativity in Workshop 1, go on to respond to the symbolism, the story, and the ideas it contains. For each workshop, encourage discussion of ideas about Christmas and the meaning of the nativity for the children and for Christians.

Workshop 2/3A (Curriculum link: Literacy)

Take the story on from the point in time shown in the painting, or write about what might have led up to it for one of the groups of characters, such as the shepherds, angels or wise men. Alternatively, begin or continue the writing (from Workshop 1) from the point of view of one of the characters. For example, 'If I were Mary…'

Workshop 2/3B (Curriculum link: Literacy, Thinking and questioning)

Imagine the future for Jesus. Tell the story using either *Godly Play Volume 3* or *Bible Storybags*. Both versions hint at what is to come in the future. Discuss the questions at the end of the story. Encourage the children to generate their own wondering questions, especially about what the future held for Jesus. Write on pieces of coloured paper or sticky notes and make a wall of questions.

Workshop 2/3C (Curriculum link: Numeracy, Thinking and questioning)

As a class, look at various pictures of angels. Compare different depictions of angels and note similarities and differences. Then work in groups to decide on categories into which you can sort the pictures. You need to be able to justify your decisions. Share your results with one other group.

Workshop 2/3D
(Curriculum link: Literacy, Art)

Read *On Angel's Wings* by Michael Morpurgo (Egmont Books, 2006). Respond with writing or art to the story.

Workshop 2/3E
(Curriculum link: Music, Science)

Show a painting of the nativity that includes musical instruments. Ask the children if they can see the instruments. Explore how musical instruments make their sounds, particularly the brass section (angels' trumpets). Listen to a recording of trumpets playing. Ask, 'I wonder why angels might play trumpets?'

Listen to music written to portray the events in the picture and make a mind map of feelings and responses as everyone listens to the music. Use colour as well as words to represent feelings. (For examples and explanation of mind-mapping, see the web link on page 95.) Ask, 'I wonder what the composer does to create atmosphere?'

Workshop 2/3F
(Curriculum link: Geography)

Map the journeys of Christmas. You could make different scales and types of map depending on whose journey it was, such as the shepherds from the hills to Bethlehem, the holy family's escape to Egypt, and so on.

Workshop 2/3G (Curriculum link: Art)

Choose from one of the following activities.

- Discuss the relevance of the story today, or what it would be like if the story happened now. Modernise an old painting of the story by adding contemporary objects and people, or by moving it to a modern setting.
- Design and create a nameplate for Jesus or a birth congratulations card. Show examples and explain to the children that they will need to show aspects of Jesus' life and his importance to Christians in their designs.
- Magnify one section of the painting and remake it in collage, paint or another medium. Divide the painting into sections and ask individuals, groups or a class to reproduce and enlarge one section each. The work can then be reassembled and displayed in the hall for whole-school worship.
- Explore ways in which the holy family has been represented by artists, using symbolism, colour, and so on. Make a holy family sculpture using paper, modroc, clay or junk.

Workshop 2/3H
(Curriculum link: DT, Maths)

Choose from one of the following activities.

- Talk about the animals in the stable that witnessed Jesus' birth, and all the visitors. Make 3D animals to be placed in the stable, such as sheep, camels, and oxen.
- Explain that the holy family needed to escape to Egypt once they had been warned by God. Invent a new travel machine to take the holy family safely to Egypt.
- Make mathematical models of stars.

Workshop 2/3I (Curriculum link: Drama)

Either hot-seat characters from the painting or use a conscience alley activity to explore various questions that arise from the story, such as 'Should the shepherds leave their sheep? Should the wise men go back to Herod's court? Should the innkeeper give Mary and Joseph a room?' and so on. As a class, discuss some of the thoughts that might have gone through the chosen characters' heads as they decided what to do. Encourage the children to think deeply about this and use their knowledge of the story.

Alternatively, debate whether giving presents is the best way to remember the meaning of Christmas. Prepare arguments for and against.

Choices for Foundation Stage linked to Areas of Learning

- Read the story using an interactive book such as *Nativity Flap Book* (Usborne, 2013) or *Touchy-Feely Nativity* (Usborne, 2008), and talk about it.

- Dress up as the characters and act out the story, or tell the story with puppets, Playmobil® or small-world characters.
- Make printed angels, using handprints for wings.
- Place the story in order from pictures.

Reflection for all choices in Workshops 2 and 3

Provide a laminated speech bubble, thought cloud and feeling heart shapes for each group. Older children or adults can scribe for younger children. Discuss and then write ideas about what one of the characters might say, what you think about the story or a character in it or its meaning, and how you or a character in the story feels.

'My Journey' reflection

Children need to complete the 'My Journey' reflection book during this session or during the next school day. On a small piece of paper, children should draw a picture or symbol to illustrate their Christmas journey, and write the date next to it. They then cut out and stick the drawing or symbol on to the timeline in the 'My Journey' book.

Generate an open or interesting question about the story and write it in the reflection book. Alternatively, ask children to answer the following question in their book: 'What is the key moment of the story and why does it matter?' Use scribes if necessary (it is important that a copy of the child's thoughts is included in the book in order for them to see their journey). Children should share their thoughts with a partner.

Whole-school worship

Preparation

Bring artwork together and display as much of it as possible. If a version of the picture has been made from small sections, reassemble and display it. Set up a focal point by showing images of your chosen painting on an IWB. Along the front of the hall, have dark fabrics draped along the floor and a bowl of stars.

Engagement

Ask the children to imagine that everyone could go to the stable. What would you see? What would you notice? Suggest that it might be the light around the stable, the noise of animals, the gifts from the wise men, Mary and Joseph or the baby in the manger. Say that above the stable, out of the darkness, shines a star—a sign that Jesus, the light for the world, has been born. For Christians, this is still a sign of God's love for the world.

Play some quiet music while two children from each class (more if appropriate or time allows) walk to the front, take a handful of stars from the bowl and sprinkle them on the dark fabric, transforming its appearance.

Reflection

As the stars are sprinkled, invite everyone to think about how our lives can be transformed and how we can transform the lives of others. A child from each class can bring an example of work done during the workshops and share it with the rest of the school, saying why it is important or special for the Christmas story.

Prayer

Use the children's prayers or choose a prayer from *The Lion Book of 1000 Prayers for Children* (pages 879–897).

Spend a few moments saying 'thank you' for the things everyone has enjoyed today (ask for suggestions from the children about what they would like to say 'thank you' for). Write the suggestions on silver stars for children to place on the fabric. Conclude with a prayer to say 'thank you' for all that has been done and shared together.

Sing a seasonal carol that the children know.

Blessing

May the angels' delight,
the shepherds' amazement,
the wise men's thirst for knowledge,
Mary and Joseph's resilience and
the Christ child's peace and love
be ours this Christmas season and always. Amen

BARBARA MEARDON

Unit 5 extension material

Class collective worship

The collective worship for this unit is designed to take place at the beginning of the spring term. The nativity story is full of journeys. Recap the journey day and talk about how sharing the journey helped you to think about the story in new ways. Ask, 'I wonder if it changed what you thought at Christmas itself?' Allow time for the children to share their memories of the day.

Look at a picture of the flight into Egypt by an artist such as J.D. Paterson, Vittore Carpaccio, Giotto, Robert T. Barrett or He Qi.

Reflection

Ask, 'I wonder what it was like for Mary and Joseph to go on that journey, leaving everything they knew and thinking about living as refugees in Egypt? I wonder what it is like for refugees now? I wonder what it is like for new children arriving at our school, or for families arriving in our town or church?'

Response

Think about new starts such as a new year and a new term. Children can write or draw their hopes, dreams and thoughts on a thought bubble.

Prayer

Heavenly Father, in the same way that the star led the wise men to Bethlehem, may the light of your presence guide us on our journeys. Amen

Looking back on the journey

Using the season of Epiphany to reflect on your experience of the Christmas story, plan a time of reflection on the theme for staff, governors and church visitors. Display a lit candle.

Response

Ask, 'I wonder how sharing the journey day has helped you to think about the story in new ways? I wonder if the day enabled you or the children to use your gifts differently?' Together, share some experiences including reactions from the children.

Display a picture of the flight into Egypt and think about the next journey in the story. Read Matthew 2:19–23.

Reflection

Ask, 'I wonder what it was like for Mary and Joseph to go on that journey, leaving everything they knew and thinking about living as refugees in Egypt? I wonder what it is like for refugees now? I wonder what it is like for new children arriving at our school, or for families arriving in our town or church?' Think about new starts, such as a new year or a new term, and reflect on what happens next in your journey as an individual or as a community, who you support and who supports you on that journey.

Invite everyone to write their hopes on a card and place it by the candle.

Prayer or blessing

Heavenly Father, as the star led the wise men, may the radiance of your presence be a light to our path, that we may come to your presence and walk before you as children of light, through Jesus Christ our Lord. Amen

Unit 5 church-based activity day

This can be a full day, half day or after-school club session.

Setting the scene

Use Christmas baubles, some candles and a manger full of straw as a focal point. If desired, display the picture you've been looking at and play some seasonal music. Display a Bible timeline such as *The Big Bible Storybook Timeline*.

Tell the story of Christmas in a reflective style (see, for example, *Bible Storybags* or *Godly Play Volume 3*).

Suggested activities

- Display Christmas cards with the words 'Peace on earth' in the design. Ask, 'I wonder what "peace on earth" means?' Children can write thoughts and questions on brightly coloured pieces of paper or sticky notes.
- Tell the story either with small play characters or by using role play in the group.
- Display examples of icons and triptychs. Explain what they are and where they might be seen. Use pieces of card or board to make an icon of the nativity. Cut out pictures of faces or people from Christmas cards. Glue them on the card and then paint or draw a border. Explain that an icon's frame is seen by some Christians as a 'window to God'. To make a triptych, score two vertical hinges on the card so that the outer flaps can be closed. Cut out faces or people as before and glue them to the centre section of the card. Decorate the outer flaps quite plainly and then open them to reveal the inner picture (the 'mystery').
- Create a Christmas stained-glass window. Either work on one large design or make individual designs. The designs can be either pre-printed or made from scratch.
- Create freeze-frames of different parts of the Christmas story. Decide which part of the story to look at and share out roles. Work out how to play the characters and how they would act during different parts of the story. When the freeze-frames are complete, touch the shoulder of each character in turn and ask them to share the thoughts and feelings of their character at that point in the story.
- Write a recipe for a perfect Christmas. Think of the ingredients you would need and how you would mix everything together.
- Look at the Christmas 'Blob' cartoon and explore associated questions (see *Blob Spirituality* by Pip Wilson).

Make or bring and share food together and say or sing a grace.

Worship

Teach a suitable Christmas carol or song for all-age worship.

Share a story that relates to the season, such as *The Fourth Wise Man* retold by Susan Summers (Dial, 1998) or by Mary Joslin (Lion, 2006) and then sing the carol 'In the bleak midwinter'. Highlight the words in the last verse and reflect on what each of us can bring.

Give each person a star shape and ask them to write their own prayer for Christmas on it. Play some seasonal music and invite everyone to place the stars on a board or piece of display paper.

UNIT 6

Jump into a picture: Easter

Bible focus

Mark 11:1–11, 15–19
Mark 14:10–72
Mark 15—16

Programme for the day

9.00–9.30am	Whole-school introduction to the day
9.30–10.35am	Workshop 1
10.35–10.55am	Break
10.55–12.00	Workshops 2 and 3 (combined)
12.00–1.00pm	Lunch
1.00–1.15pm (or next day)	'My Journey' reflection
1.15–2.20pm	Workshops 2 and 3 (continued)
2.20–2.30pm	Break
2.30–3.00pm	Whole-school worship

Preparation

Plan a time of reflection on the theme for staff, governors and church visitors. Either have a small copy of the Easter story picture to be used in the journey day for each person to hold or project the picture on an IWB. The suggested picture is *The Last Supper* by Simon Smith, a large laminated poster showing part of the Easter story but with symbols or pictures of much of the rest of the Holy Week and Jesus' life and ministry. The poster is available from Blackburn Diocesan Board of Education (see web link, page 95).

Response

Ask, 'I wonder how you feel about this picture? I wonder how you feel about the journey ahead of you this year? I wonder whether any of the ideas or images in the painting has anything to say about your journey?'

Share ideas in groups, in pairs, or by each person writing a thought on a flower, Easter egg or cross shape and placing the shape around a lit candle. Conclude the reflection with a short silence or with quiet music, such as *Miserere Mei* by Allegri or *Fantasia on a Theme by Thomas Tallis* by Vaughan Williams.

Read Mark 11:1–10.

Blessing

We ask your blessing on all our preparations for this part of our journey, and on the day itself, that walking alongside each other we will learn more about you and about each other and grow as a community together. Amen

Whole-school introduction to the day

As a focal point, display filled plastic Easter eggs (see below), a cross, lengths of black, yellow or white fabric draped together and some palm crosses. As the children come into the hall, play the mp3 track 'Sing Alleluia' by Jennifer Knapp and Mac Powell (see YouTube) or play *Fantasia on a Theme by Thomas Tallis*.

Reflection

Show a copy of *The Last Supper* by Simon Smith on an IWB. Ask, 'I wonder who the characters represented in this painting are?' Explain that the painting is about the last week of Jesus' life. Ask, 'I wonder which event in that week the painting is about? I wonder what question you would like to ask someone in the painting?'

Explain that Christians call the last week of Jesus' life 'Holy Week', and that the rest of the day will be spent thinking about the events of that week.

Storytelling

Tell the story of Holy Week using hollow plastic eggs filled with the symbols below. Invite volunteers to choose an egg, open it and tell everyone what is inside.

- A palm leaf (Palm Sunday)
- A coin (cleansing the temple)
- Some bread (the last supper)

- Praying hands (the garden of Gethsemane)
- A tiny sword (Jesus is arrested by soldiers)
- A crown of thorns (Jesus is on trial)
- A cross (Jesus is killed)
- An empty egg (the empty tomb on Easter Day)

Explain that the children will come back together at the end of the day to share what they have found out about Holy Week and Easter on their journey.

Play the PowerPoint or mp3 track of 'Sing Alleluia' again, or use other seasonal music, as the children go out. Use the picture, focus and questions to make a reflection corner in school or church. (For ideas, see the *Pause for Reflection* pack.)

Learning intention (for all workshops)

Children explore the story and symbolism in the picture and how this expresses the meaning of the story for Christians.

The following areas of focus are suggested. (This will not apply if you are using vertical/family groupings.)

- Foundation Stage and Year 1: Palm Sunday
- Years 2 and 3: Easter Sunday and new life
- Year 4: The last supper
- Year 5: Jesus' trial and Good Friday
- Year 6: The garden of Gethsemane, the arrest and Peter's denial

Workshop 1: Exploring the picture

Engagement

Choose a painting showing the part of the Easter story that you are considering. Display it on the IWB. When choosing a painting, think about what the children will be able to see and understand or find out about (see the 'I wonder' questions below).

The National Gallery has a number of classical paintings on its website. Another good web-based gallery is 'Joyful Heart', which also includes some modern paintings (see web link, page 95).

You might like to consider artists who have painted a series to show the Easter story. For example, Sieger Köder, James J. Tissot (French impressionist painter, 1836–1902) and Tintoretto (1518–94) all have amazing series of paintings covering the whole of Holy Week (see web links, page 95). Tintoretto's list includes:

- The Last Supper (c. 1593), oil on canvas, S. Giorgio Maggiore, Venice
- The Last Supper (1578–81), oil on canvas, Scuola di San Rocco, Venice
- Jesus Going to the Mount of Olives at Night
- Man Bearing a Pitcher
- Judas Goes to the Chief Priests
- The Pharisees Conspire Together
- Jesus Washes the Feet of the Disciples
- Last Discourse of Our Lord Jesus
- Judas Retires from the Supper
- The Last Supper
- Communion of the Apostles (shows Jesus serving bread as a priest to communicants)
- The Jews' Passover

Ask 'I wonder' questions:

- I wonder which part of the story is depicted in the picture?
- I wonder how the artist has expressed it?

Discuss and generate questions to explore the story and the painting. Can you make connections with other stories in other parts of the Bible? Look at the symbolism used to depict the characters or object you are focusing on. Ask, 'I wonder how this helps you understand the story of Easter?'

If you are using *The Last Supper* by Simon Smith, you could use the set of cards that accompanies it (see web link, page 95) and give one or more to each child, asking them to find their person or object and then talk about how they fit into the story.

Response

Choose one of the following activities.

- In small groups, look at other examples of the same part of the story in paintings, sculpture or stained glass. Look for similarities and differences and share your findings with the class.
- Write individual or class poetry—for example, an acrostic, where each line begins with a letter from an appropriate word such as RESURRECTION, EASTER, or HE IS RISEN, or a kenning, where each line describes what you are talking about without ever saying what it is (for example, Jesus is a death defier, a saviour, a joy bringer, and so on).
- Write a narrative in response to the story as one of the characters at the first Easter: choose from Mary, Jesus, one of the criminals, Peter, a Roman soldier and Pontius Pilate. Write in the first person, as if you are describing events as they happen, and ensure that you talk about thoughts and feelings as well as events. This activity could be continued in Workshop 2.

Reflection for all Workshop 1 choices

Look at the main painting for the day, *The Last Supper* by Simon Smith. Can you find anything that links to the part of the Holy Week story that we are looking at? For example, for Palm Sunday you can see a donkey, Jerusalem and the temple through the window, or for Good Friday you can see the nails, a curtain and a lamb.

Workshops 2 and 3 (combined): Creative response to the picture

Note: Either choose one workshop to cover both time slots or two different workshops. Continue with the same painting as you used for Workshop 1. Whichever workshop is chosen, the reflection is the same (see page 67).

Workshops 2/3A to 2/3E are suitable for all-age groups. Workshops 2/3F onwards are specific to different age groups. As in Workshop 1, the suggested parts of the story to explore for different age groups are:

- Foundation Stage and Year 1: Palm Sunday
- Years 2 and 3: Easter Day and new life
- Year 4: The last supper
- Year 5: Jesus' trial and Good Friday
- Year 6: The garden of Gethsemane, the arrest and Peter's denial

Workshop 2/3A (Curriculum link: Literacy)

Take the story on from the point in time shown in the painting, or write about what might have led up to it for one of the groups of characters—for example, the Roman soldiers, the disciples or Jesus' family.

Alternatively, begin or continue the writing (from Workshop 1) from the point of view of one of the characters—for example, 'Imagine if I were Mary…' Write in the first person as if you are describing events as they happen, and ensure that you talk about thoughts and feelings as well as events.

Workshop 2/3B (Curriculum link: Literacy, Thinking and questioning)

Retell the story using figures and reflective storytelling (from *Godly Play Volume 4*, *Bible Storybags* or *The Big Bible Storybook*). Encourage the children to generate their own 'I wonder' questions about the disciples' future. Write them on pieces of coloured paper or sticky notes and make a wall of questions.

Alternatively, watch clips of your part of the Easter story on the BBC learning zone (see web links, page 95).

Workshop 2/3C (Curriculum link: Art, History, Geography, DT)

Choose from the following alternatives:

- Modernise the painting.
- Magnify one section of the painting or divide it into sections, then enlarge each section to make one very large class version.
- Make individual pictures or sculptures to show your part of the Easter story.
- Make a series of same-size pictures/sculptures which, when assembled, will tell the whole story of Holy Week and Easter. See McCrimmons' set of pictures, *Jesus our Way*, for ideas.

Workshop 2/3D (Curriculum link: DT, History, Numeracy)

Make 3D models of specific objects, people and/or buildings in your part of the story.

Workshop 2/3E (Curriculum link: Drama, Thinking skills)

Choose from the following alternatives:

- Hot-seat characters from the painting.
- Use a conscience alley activity to explore various aspects of the story. For example, in Year 5 (Jesus' trial) you could use this workshop to look at Pilate's decision. As a class, discuss some of the thoughts that might have gone through the chosen characters' heads as they decided what to do. Encourage the children to think deeply about this and use their knowledge of the story.
- Debate the characters' decision: prepare arguments for and against, or use PMI to discuss the questions.

Workshop 2/3F

This workshop is specific to Foundation Stage/Year 1.

Offer a rotation of activities related to Palm Sunday, to include a range of the following:

- Any suitable activities from Workshops 2/3A to 2/3E.
- Read the story from *The Big Bible Storybook*.
- Dress up as the characters and act out the story.
- Tell the story with puppets or Playmobil™ or small-world characters.
- Tell the story by arranging pictures in order.
- Show pictures of what the walls and gate of Jerusalem might have looked like, then build a model from a choice of materials—for example, blocks, Lego™ or junk boxes.
- Draw memory jogger pictures for each part of the story and use them to retell the story.
- Make palm leaves from coloured paper or card.
- Learn and sing a Palm Sunday song, adding percussion.
- Use collage to create a large picture of Jesus arriving on the donkey.
- Decorate cardboard crosses with greenery, leaves, rosemary, and so on.

Workshop 2/3G (Curriculum link: Thinking and reasoning, Art, DT, Literacy)

This workshop is specific to Years 2 and 3.

Recap the story of Easter Day by reading a children's version—for example, *The Easter Bible Storybook* by Maggie Barfield, *Easter: The Everlasting Story* by Lois Rock or *Easter* by Brian Wildsmith. You could use the reflective storytelling method from *Bible Storybags* or *Godly Play Volume 4*.

Learn a Christian song or hymn about Easter to share at whole-school worship later. Then, through a rotation of activities across the two workshops, explore the story using any suitable activities in Workshops 2/3A to E, or use any of the following activities, which explore how Christians celebrate Easter now. You could use a combination of the two.

Easter services

Find out about Easter services in church, including special celebratory music (available from CDs or iTunes), responses ('Christ is risen. Alleluia. He is risen indeed. Alleluia') and the Paschal candle. Show some photographs, look in the books and websites (see web links on page 95, particularly 'Sophie's Easter' on the BBC learning zone) and interview the visitors from church. Think about how the people at the service feel and what each aspect of the service is trying to show you about the Easter story and its meaning.

Response

Make a mind map to gather your information together, with different colours showing different pieces of information, feelings and meanings.

Colours and sunrise

Find out about how colour is used in the church (both Anglican and Orthodox traditions) at Easter. Ask, 'I wonder how this helps Christians celebrate Easter? I wonder how it links to the Easter story and its meaning?' Design an altar frontal, banner or vestments for an Easter service.

Find out about sunrise walks and services—for example, the Taizé sunrise service. Ask, 'I wonder why Christians celebrate Easter this way. I wonder how it links to the Easter story and its meaning.'

Response

Plan an Easter sunrise service, thinking about where it would take place in your area, when it should happen and what you would do, or write a 'recipe' for a sunrise service—for example, 'Very early in the morning before the sun has risen, take one spoon of excitement, one cup of friendship, some quiet moments of prayer...' and so on.

Easter gardens

Look at pictures of Easter gardens. Ask, 'I wonder how this helps Christians celebrate Easter? I wonder how it links to the Easter story and its meaning?'

Response

Make or design an Easter garden individually or as a group.

Easter foods

Research the special foods eaten at Easter time and the meaning of the traditions behind them—hot cross buns, simnel cake, roast lamb and, of course, Easter eggs. You could look at international customs—Czech babobka and Polish baba (sweet cakes); Syrian and Jordanian honey pastries; Italian pretzels (shaped to indicate the torso of a person with arms folded, praying) and colomba (bread shaped like a dove to symbolise spring, Christ and peace); Russian blinis (little pancakes).

Find out about different ways of decorating Easter eggs, such as Ukrainian *krashanky* and *pysanky* eggs, Russian Fabergé eggs or Polish wooden painted eggs.

Find out about different egg-related Easter games. Egg rolling races are held all over the world on Easter Monday. Eggs are rolled down a hill or slope and the first one to reach the bottom without breaking is the winner. There is also an egg-knocking game played in several countries, including France, Germany, Norway and Syria. The game is played with hard-boiled eggs and is a bit like 'conkers'. The object of the game is to hit everyone else's egg and to keep your own one unbroken. The last player with a whole egg is declared the winner. Ask, 'I wonder how this reminds us of the Easter story?' (answers might include the tomb being 'cracked' open and Jesus being alive).

Response

Make hot cross buns or Easter biscuits that are cut in symbolic shapes, such as eggs, butterflies, crosses and so on. Talk about how making special foods can help us to think about the story and what it means.

Easter cards

Collect a selection of Easter cards and sort them into categories, explaining why you have sorted them the way you did. Ask, 'I wonder which cards help Christians celebrate Easter? I wonder which ones link to the Easter story and its meaning?'

Response

Design and/or make an Easter card using symbols that link to the Easter story and its meaning. You can create your own design, use black scratch cards (revealing bright colours underneath), or make a cross-shaped card and decorate it with flowers to show the transformation of the sad news of Good Friday to the happiness of resurrection on Easter Day.

Spring flowers

Find out about the flowers associated with spring and Easter festivals. Some flowers have been given special meanings by Christians to help them celebrate Easter. White lilies, for example, represent purity and goodness, helping Christians to remember that Jesus was pure and perfect when he died on the cross.

Other significant flowers are the pussy willow (UK, Finland and Russia), daffodils (Europe, especially southern France and Italy), and passion flowers, which represent a number of different things for Christians. The three stamens of the passion flower represent the three nail wounds of Jesus or the Trinity of God, Jesus and the Holy Spirit, or the three crosses. The circle of petals represents the crown of thorns that Jesus wore. As there are ten petals, these can represent the ten disciples who did not deny or betray Christ. The leaves represent the spear that went into the side of Jesus. The passion flower normally lasts for three days and represents the three days that Jesus spent in the tomb.

Response

Paint or draw the Easter flowers and say what they symbolise, or make paper flowers and stick them on to a large bare cross made from two big cardboard tubes with slits down the centre, joined to make a cross.

Easter around the world

Find out how Easter is celebrated in different parts of the world (see web link, page 95). Ask, 'I wonder how this helps Christians celebrate Easter? I wonder how it links to the Easter story and its meaning?'

Response

Choose your favourite custom, draw a picture and/or write about it on a memory jogger card so that you can tell someone else about the custom and how it helps you to understand the Easter story and its meaning.

Butterflies

Read *The Very Hungry Caterpillar* by Eric Carle and then talk about how caterpillars change into butterflies. They are the same but different—transformed. Christians use this image to help them to understand the resurrection.

Response

Make a butterfly by using a method that involves transformation—for example, using beads that can then be ironed (by an adult) to fuse them together, or wax resist and colour wash techniques. Information to help you do this can be found on the internet.

Useful resources

- *Easter Sparkler Celebrations* by Katie Dicker
- *Easter: My Family Celebrates* by Cath Senker
- *Why Do We Celebrate Easter?* by Mark Sutherland
- Web links on page 95

Workshop 2/3H (Curriculum link: Art, DT)

This workshop is specific to Year 4.

Watch one or more of the short clips from the BBC learning zone that tell the story of the Last Supper (including a cartoon version and one where children act out the Last Supper). Generate questions for the people or characters in the film clips. Show the painting *The Last Supper* by Sieger Köder.

Through a rotation of activities across the two workshops, explore the story using any suitable activities in Workshops A to E, or use the following activities, which explore connections between the Last Supper, Jewish Passover, Communion and Maundy Thursday in the church today. You could use a combination of the two.

At the end of the rotations, you could act out the Last Supper using unleavened bread (the bread you have made or matzos biscuits) and some blackcurrant squash or grape juice.

Communion

Show a three-minute 'Learning zone' clip from the BBC and a PowerPoint presentation on a laptop or IWB. Alternatively, for use with Key Stage 1 children, see resources from www.nottsopenchurches.org.uk and www.request.org.uk (see web links, page 95).

Explain that something that all churches do is the sharing of Communion, the breaking of bread. If the adult at the table has experienced a Communion service in a different culture, they could share that experience. A painting that illustrates this is *All are welcome* by Sieger Köder. Ask, 'I wonder how this helps Christians to celebrate the Last Supper on Maundy Thursday? I wonder how it links to the story of the Last Supper and its meaning?' Look at a chalice and paten. Ask, 'I wonder if you can see any links with the painting we are looking at today?'

Response

Print off large individual letters to spell out the words 'Remember me', and ask the children to draw a small picture or symbol in each letter to represent something that would help people to remember the story of the Last Supper.

Washing feet

Bring a bowl of water and a towel, and talk about washing feet. Ask, 'I wonder if anyone would like their feet washed? I wonder if anybody would like to do the foot washing?'

Once the children have had the experience, whether by taking part or watching, discuss how it felt to watch or to have their feet washed, or to be the foot washer. Then tell the children that before they ate the last supper together, Jesus washed his disciples' feet. Look at paintings of this event, such as *The washing of feet* by Sieger Köder. Ask, 'I wonder why Jesus washed their feet? I wonder how the disciples felt? I wonder what this tells us about the kind of leader that Jesus was?'

On Maundy Thursday, when Christians remember the Last Supper, they sometimes take part in foot washing. Ask, 'I wonder how this helps Christians to celebrate the Last Supper on Maundy Thursday? I wonder how it links to the painting we are looking at today, or to the story of the Last Supper and its meaning?'

Response

Design a poster for the class, showing how we can serve other people.

Unleavened bread

Think carefully about what you have already found out about the Last Supper, and look carefully at the picture of the Last Supper. Ask, 'I wonder what kind of food they are eating? I wonder what we'd need to make if we were to act out the Last Supper this afternoon? I wonder what you notice about the break in the painting?'

Response

Make unleavened bread and talk about why it is unleavened, linking to the story of the Passover (Exodus 12).

You will need:

- 300 g plain flour
- 112 ml water
- 15 ml olive oil
- Pinch of salt

Mix all ingredients together and knead for 5–10 minutes until a soft dough is formed (add tiny amounts of extra water or flour if the consistency is not right). Cut into six pieces, then roll out or flatten with hands to be as flat as possible. Prick all over with a fork. Bake in a hot oven (220°C/Gas Mark 7) for 5–6 minutes.

Maundy money

Find out about the tradition of the Queen giving Maundy money at special services on Maundy Thursday. Centuries ago, the reigning king or queen would wash the feet of a small number of poor people, the number of people being the same as the monarch's age. This helped them to remember that Jesus washed his disciples' feet before the last supper. Nowadays the Queen, carrying a small pomander or bouquet of sweet herbs, gives little purses of money to a few chosen men and women. The coins are special little silver pennies and the purses are made of soft leather, closed with a drawstring. The ceremony is held at Westminster Abbey, in London, every other year. In the years when it isn't held at Westminster Abbey, the Queen distributes the Maundy money at different cathedrals in the country.

Watch a BBC video clip of the Queen distributing Maundy money (see web link, page 95). Ask, 'I wonder how this helps Christians to celebrate the Last Supper on Maundy Thursday? I wonder how it links to the painting we are looking at today and the story of the Last Supper and its meaning?'

Ask the visitor from church what happens at their Maundy Thursday services. The Maundy money is symbolic of serving others: what other symbols are there?

Workshop 2/3I (Curriculum link: Literacy, Science, Geography)

This workshop is specific to Year 5.

Show the children the Good Friday page on the Woodland Junior School website (web link, page 95).

Through a rotation of activities across the two workshops, explore the story using any suitable activities in Workshops A to E, or use the following activities, which explore the events, meaning and significance of Good Friday. You could use a combination of the two.

Arrest and trial

Imagine you are either a webpage designer or a team of reporters from the BBC Newsround website who have to cover the arrest and trial of Jesus.

Response

Decide what you need to write about in order to explain the events to someone who was not there. You might think about what are the most important aspects to report, what sort of debate there might be on the website, whether you need to represent what happens from different viewpoints, who you would interview and why. You can present your ideas as a storyboard or on the computer.

Passion flower

Think about the passion flower as a symbol of the events of Good Friday. Looking at real passion flowers or photographs, generate questions or ideas about how the passion flower could represent Good Friday (see information on page 63, under 'Spring flowers'). Then look at the explanation on www.whyeaster.com and compare it with your ideas. Were your questions answered? When you do the reflection at the end of the workshop, think about Jesus or one of the robbers.

Response

Draw and label a passion flower to show the symbolic meaning.

Passion plays and Good Friday services

How is Good Friday remembered by Christians in church now? Explore what happens in churches on Good Friday (ask your church visitor what your local church does)—for example, a children's workshop at church, walk of witness with a cross, three-hour vigil, words from the cross with special music.

Look at pictures of various passion plays, such as *The Way of the Cross* in Salisbury, Wintershall, Oberammergau, York, or the *Way of the Cross* in Jerusalem. Ask the children what they think the pictures show. Then explain that a passion play is a re-enactment of the events of Holy Week.

Response

Thinking about your own village/town or school, plan where and how you could stage the trial and Good Friday events. Once you have decided on the key events to cover, divide up tasks in your group to look at costumes and props; locations and staging; music; dialogue or action.

Stations of the cross

Show a picture of a railway station, and ask what a station is. Explain what a station of the cross is—a chance to pause on your journey and think about an event in Jesus' journey to the cross.

Look at pictures from the Way of the Cross in Jerusalem and various examples of stations of the cross—

stained glass, sculpture, plaques and paintings. The poster sets available from McCrimmons, *A Way of the Cross for Children: The Footsteps of Christ*, would also be useful. Discuss how each one helps you to understand what is happening. How has the artist conveyed meaning and feelings?

Response

Choose one of the stations and design a poster for it, ensuring that you show meaning and feelings.

Workshop 2/3J (Curriculum link: Literacy)

This workshop is specific to Year 6.

Show the BBC learning zone clip of the crucifixion and Peter's denial (see web link, page 95). Set up a rotation of five activities in the classroom to explore the story further.

Garden of Gethsemane

Listen to the Taizé song 'Stay with me, keep watch with me', and look at a painting of Jesus and the disciples in the garden of Gethsemane—for example, by Sieger Köder or Tissot. Ask, 'I wonder how the artist and the composer captured some of the meaning of this part of the Easter story? I wonder what it was like for the disciples? I wonder if it is possible to imagine how Jesus felt?'

Response

Imagine that you were there, and brainstorm words that express your feelings. Using some of your feeling words and what you know about the story and its meaning for Christians, write a script to retell the story and compose some music that conveys the serious atmosphere of this time in the garden. Retell the story with the musical accompaniment.

Watchnight services

In the garden of Gethsemane, Jesus asked the disciples to pray with him. He asked the disciples to share that time of prayer with him, but they fell asleep. Christians today have special services called 'watchnight' services and times of prayer on Maundy Thursday to remember this part of the story and to keep watch and pray in preparation for Good Friday and Easter.

Response

Design a watchnight service that will help people to wait and pray.

Jesus' arrest

Think about the arrest in the garden, look at paintings, compare the accounts in the Gospels and identify the key points of the story. Create a series of freeze frames to show each of these points. At each freeze frame, pause and reflect on what the characters are feeling and their part in the story.

Show a clip of the arrest in the garden from an Easter passion play or the DVD of *The Miracle Maker*.

Response

Write a review for a Christian newspaper or webpage, including comments on how accurate it is and whether it would help Christians to understand the events of the story and their meaning.

Peter's denial (1)

Read about Peter's denial in the Gospels or a suitable children's Bible, such as *The Bible in 365 Stories*. Watch the BBC learning zone clip about this part of the story (see web link, page 95). Ask, 'I wonder if you can think of a time when you let a friend down? How did you feel? Were you able to do anything about it?'

Restorative justice is a way for people who have done something wrong to make amends by talking or writing to the person they have hurt.

Response

Write a letter from Peter to Jesus to express his sorrow, shame and regret at his actions, making sure that you include details for the story that you have read. Finish by reading John 21:15–17, which describes what happened after Jesus rose again, and discuss how Peter's feelings might have changed as a result.

Peter's denial (2)

Use conscience alley or PMI to decide how Peter should have acted when he was recognised by the people round the fire. Should he have denied Jesus or admitted that he knew him? Ask, 'I wonder, if Peter had used one of these techniques, would he have made a different decision? I wonder if this gives you a better understanding of the story and its meaning?'

Response

Write a short piece about what might have happened to Peter if he hadn't denied knowing Jesus.

Reflection for all Workshop 2/3 choices

Provide a laminated speech bubble, thought cloud and feeling heart shapes for each group. Older children or adults can scribe for younger children. Discuss, then write ideas about what one of the characters might say, what you think about the story or a character in it or its meaning, and how you or a character in the story feels.

'My Journey' reflection

On a small piece of paper, children should draw a picture or symbol to illustrate their Easter journey, write the date next to it, cut it out and stick it on to the timeline in their 'My Journey' book. Ask children to generate an open or interesting question about the story and write it in the book or answer the following question: 'What is the key moment of the story, and why does it matter?'

Use scribes if necessary: it is important that a copy of the child's thoughts is included in the book in order for them to see their journey. Share thoughts with a partner.

Whole-school worship

Preparation

Bring artwork together and display as much as possible. If a version of the picture has been made from small sections, this will need to be reassembled. On an IWB, show an image of the main painting used for the day.

As the children arrive, show the PowerPoint presentation or play the mp3 track 'Sing Alleluia' by Jennifer Knapp and Mac Powell.

Engagement

Say, 'Imagine if we could be there that first Easter morning. The dew is on the grass, and the sun is shining. I wonder how you would feel if you saw Jesus in the garden? I wonder who you would rush to tell? Christians all around the world celebrate Easter with shouts of joy and Easter greetings.'

Sing a song, such as 'Sing Alleluia'.

Say, 'Today we have explored the story of the whole of Holy Week and Easter. Let's share the story together.'

Repeat the telling of the Easter story, using the hollow plastic eggs from the morning session, but this time open them in the correct order of the story of Easter. Invite a child from the class that has looked at a particular part of the story to open the appropriate egg and say what the object inside is and what it represents.

Then, children from that class can bring an example of work done during the workshops and share it with the rest of the school, explaining why it is important or special for the Easter story and for Christians today.

Prayer

Use prayers written by the children in their workshops or taken from *The Lion Book of 1000 Prayers for Children* (pages 455–461).

Explain that you are going to have a time of giving thanks for the things you've enjoyed today. Ask the children what they would like to say 'thank you' for. Say a prayer of thanks for 'all that we've been able to do and share together'.

Teach this blessing with actions, then all join in together.

May God's Holy Spirit be in your life
  (hand on heart)
May God's Holy Spirit be in our world
  (sweep hand out in front)
May God's Holy Spirit be love between us
  (hold or shake hands)
And the blessing of God Almighty, Father, Son and Holy Spirit, be among us and remain with us this day and always. Amen

REVD DR SANDRA MILLAR

Unit 6 extension material

Class collective worship

Show the picture used as a focus on the journey day to give children the opportunity to revisit the Easter story and their experiences of the day. Then tell them the story of the road to Emmaus (Luke 24:13–33), show them one of the following pictures and generate questions about it (see web links, page 95).

- *The Road to Emmaus* by HeQi.
- *Way to Emmaus* Robert Zünd (Swiss painter, 1827–1909), Kunstmuseum, St Gallen.
- *The Road to Emmaus* by Melone.

Reflection

Ask, 'I wonder if you noticed how Jesus was with the two disciples?' He drew alongside them and joined them on their journey, he listened to their story and helped them to make sense of how they felt and to decide what to do next. Christians believe that Jesus walks alongside them on their journey through life, listening to them, helping them make sense of their lives.

Response

Play some quiet reflective music, such as *Fantasy on a Theme by Thomas Tallis* by Vaughan Williams. Ask some wondering questions.

- I wonder who 'walks alongside' you on your journey through life?
- I wonder who you walk alongside?
- I wonder who helps you when you face something challenging or difficult?
- I wonder who listens to you?
- I wonder whether you help others by listening well?

Children could add thoughts, questions or responses to their 'My Journey' book about this part of their learning journey.

Prayer

Choose a prayer from *The Lion Book of 1000 Prayers for Children* (pages 455–461) or from a similar book.

Looking back on the journey

Plan a time of reflection on the theme for staff, governors and church visitors. Reflect on some of the experiences from the journey day itself or any follow-up work that has occurred within the school or the church.

Response

Have some bread and wine, a cross, a piece of white linen and cut-out footprints on display. Light a candle and reflect on the symbols of Easter and what they represent to you on your journey.

Conclude the reflection with a time of silence or listen to quiet music, followed by a blessing:

Lord, we ask to be blessed in our walking.
We ask to be blessed on the road.
We ask to be blessed drawing near.
We ask to be blessed in the listening.
We ask to be blessed in the early morning.
We ask to be blessed in the quiet evening.
We ask to be blessed in the meeting at your table.
We ask to be blessed in the sharing of the bread.
We ask to be blessed in the going out into your world.
We ask to be blessed in all the blessings that we see.
Amen

Unit 6 church-based activity day

This can be a full day, half day or after-school club session.

Setting the scene

Display a Bible timeline, such as *The Big Bible Storybook Timeline*.

Place objects to represent elements of the story—for example, sandals, walking staff, pictures of an open road in the holy land, bread and wine. You could use these objects afterwards to make a reflection corner in church. (For ideas, see the *Pause for Reflection* pack.)

Engagement

Look at a painting of Jesus walking alongside the disciples. What questions do you want to ask about the painting?

Discuss the art of conversation—the importance of using the skills of both speaking and listening. As you listen to the story, notice the way each person in it listens and speaks.

Share the story by reading from a suitable Bible or acting it out together. If you have an 'Open the Book' team, ask them to act it out.

Alternatively, the leader can tell the story while adults and children mime the actions, or you could tell the story using a series of art images to illustrate key points in the story.

Suggested activities

- Either design a menu, create table decorations and prepare food to share with friends, or taste a range of breads from around the world and look at recipes for different types of bread.
- Explore the painting:
  - Say five things you noticed about the painting…
  - Say five words to sum up or describe the painting…
  - I wonder how the painting makes you feel?
  - I wonder what you think the picture is about?
  - I wonder what the artist took from the Bible story itself?
  - I wonder if the artist added anything to the story?
  - I wonder whether you think the artist likes Jesus? I wonder how you can tell?
  - I wonder what is surprising or interesting about the painting?
  - I wonder where the church would hang the painting? Why?
- Design a modern painting to show the events of the story and its meaning for Christians. In the story, the disciples turn from despondency and confusion to joy and understanding: a transformation takes place. Can you create a piece of art on the theme of transformation or a piece of art that highlights the contrasting feelings of the disciples?
- Introduce pupils to the history of labyrinths and how they have been used as an aid to prayer and meditation. Look at a picture of the labyrinth in Chartres Cathedral and other examples. Create a labyrinth in a suitable space within the church or outside, which enables people to reflect on their life journey, their feelings and their beliefs. Provide enough time for people to walk the labyrinth and to spend time in quiet reflection. Write or draw in a reflective diary, or create a piece of artwork or music to express a significant thought, belief or event that you reflected on as you walked the labyrinth.
- Take a blindfold walk in pairs, with the sighted person describing what they see. What is it like to walk along and not see or realise what is happening? Swap roles.
- Compare the words of the Communion service with Bible references from this story and the story of Maundy Thursday.
- Make an altar frontal or banner to use at the all-age Communion. Talk about why we use these things in church and how they can help to tell stories or inspire people and be made to the glory of God.
- Learn the song 'Ewe, Thina (We Walk His Way)'. A John Bell version of this is available from iTunes. Add percussion and/or dance.

Make or bring and share food together. Say or sing grace or use one of the blessings written in the workshops.

Worship

As the disciples walked along the Emmaus road, Jesus came and joined them on their journey and walked alongside them. He helped them make sense of their situation, and, as he shared a meal with them, they recognised him.

- I wonder who 'walks alongside' you on your journey through life?
- I wonder who helps you when you face something challenging or difficult?
- I wonder who listens to you?
- Do you help others by listening well?

Suggested songs

He walked where I walk, *The Gift Songbook* (available to download from www.grahamkendrick.co.uk)
Ewe, Thina (We Walk His Way)

UNIT 7

Jump into a picture: Pentecost

Bible focus

Acts 2:1–47

Programme for the day

9.00–9.30am	Whole-school introduction to the day
9.30–10.35am	Workshop 1
10.35–10.55am	Break
10.55–12.00	Workshops 2 and 3 (combined)
12.00–1.00pm	Lunch
1.00–1.15pm (or next day)	'My Journey' reflection
1.15–2.20pm	Workshops 2 and 3 (continued)
2.20–2.30pm	Break
2.30–3.00pm	Whole-school worship

Preparation

Plan a time of reflection on the theme for the staff, governors and church volunteers. Have a small copy of the Pentecost picture to be used on the journey day for each individual to hold, or project the picture on a board.

You could choose from the following pictures (see web links, page 95).

- Turvey Abbey Pentecost Celebration Poster
- *Pentecost* by Giotto di Bondone (two paintings)
- *Peter Preaching at Pentecost* by Benjamin West (1738–1820)
- Detail from the Linaiuoli Triptych, 'Predella Showing St Peter Preaching', 1433 by Fra Angelico. This is a small panel on the bottom left of the triptych. It would be interesting to show the whole triptych.
- *Way of Light* poster set ('Pentecost') or *Power of the Spirit* poster ('Pentecost') by Sr Sheila Gosney RJM
- 'Untitled—Pentecost' by John Brokenshire (b. 1958), from the *Methodist Collection of Modern Christian Art*, No. 39
- *Whirlwind and Wellspring* by Sophie Hacker

Ask the group to look at the painting, which represents an extraordinary experience in the lives of the disciples. Within the journey of the people of God, it was the beginning of the worldwide Christian church and is celebrated today at Pentecost. Ask some wondering questions:

- I wonder how you respond to the picture?
- I wonder how you feel about the journey ahead of you this year?
- I wonder if any of the ideas or images in the painting have anything to say about your journey?

You may choose to share ideas at this point, through discussion as a group or in pairs, or each person could write a thought on a star, flower or cross shape and place it around a candle.

Spend some quiet time thinking about where you are on your journey. Conclude the reflection with a time of silence or some quiet music, followed by Bible readings from Acts 2:1–12 and Isaiah 11:1–3.

Blessing

Teach this blessing with actions, then all join in together.

May God's Holy Spirit be in your life
  (hand on heart)
May God's Holy Spirit be in our world
  (sweep hand out in front)
May God's Holy Spirit be love between us
  (hold or shake hands)
And the blessing of God Almighty, Father, Son and Holy Spirit, be among us and remain with us this day and always. Amen

REVD DR SANDRA MILLAR

Whole-school introduction to the day

As a focal point, show a copy of the picture or pictures (you may need to use more than one to convey the ideas of the whole story) on an IWB. Red, orange and yellow material draped to look like flames, with a fan blowing on them, would look good.

Play seasonal music as the children come in—for example, 'Come, Creator Spirit' by Keith Duke, available from iTunes.

Reflection

Show a painting that includes people (for example, the eleven disciples). Ask some wondering questions:

- I wonder if you know any of the characters represented in this painting? Is there anything that gives you a clue?
- I wonder what the artist has done to show you who they are? *(The answer could be as simple as haloes around the disciples' heads.)*
- I wonder if you can think of a question you'd like to ask someone in the painting?
- I wonder if you can think of a question you'd ask the artist about the painting?
- I wonder how the people in the painting are feeling at this moment in the story?

Read the Pentecost story from an appropriate Bible (see page 11).

Prayers

Choose prayers from *The Lion Book of 1000 Prayers for Children* (pages 926–928).

Explain that everyone will come back together at the end of the day to share what they have found out about Pentecost.

Sing or listen to 'Breathe on me, Breath of God' or some Taizé music, such as *Veni Sancte Spiritus* or Holy Spirit, Come to Us—*Tui Amoris Ignem*.

Use the picture, focus and questions to make a reflection corner (for ideas, see the *Pause for Reflection* pack).

Workshop 1: Exploring the picture

Learning intention

Children explore the story and symbolism in the picture and how the symbolism expresses the meaning of the story for Christians.

Engagement

Display a copy of the picture on the IWB. Ask, 'I wonder which part of the story is depicted in the picture? I wonder how the artist has expressed it?'

Discuss and generate questions to explore the story and the painting. Can you make connections with other parts of the Bible (for example, God speaking to Moses through the burning bush, or Jesus calming the wind on the lake)?

Look at the symbolism used to depict the characters or object you are focusing on. Ask, 'I wonder how this helps us understand the story of Pentecost?'

Response

Choose one of the following activities.

- In small groups, look at other examples of the same part of the story in paintings, sculpture or stained glass. Look for similarities and differences and share your findings with the class.
- Write individual or class poetry—perhaps an acrostic, in which each line begins with a letter from an appropriate word such as PENTECOST, WIND AND FLAME or SPIRIT, or a kenning, where each line describes what you are talking about without saying what it is (for example, a disciple could be 'news bringer' or 'Jesus follower'; the Spirit of God is a 'hope bringer', 'courage maker', and so on).
- Write a narrative in response to the story—for example as if you were one of the disciples at the first Pentecost. Write in the first person, describing events as they happened. Ensure that you talk about thoughts and feelings as well as events. This activity could be continued in Workshop 2.

Reflection

Share responses as a whole group or class (adults or older children could scribe). You could display responses on a board.

Workshops 2 and 3 combined: Creative response to the picture

Either choose one workshop to cover both time slots or two different workshops. Whichever workshop is chosen, the reflection is the same (see page 73).

Learning intention

Having looked at the painting of Pentecost in Workshop 1, children go on to respond to the symbolism, story and ideas it contains. In each workshop, encourage discussion of ideas about Pentecost and the meaning of the story for the children and for Christians.

To find out how Christians celebrate Pentecost now, look at www.request.org.uk (see web link, page 95). Alternatively, read the story of Pentecost at The Children's Chapel (see web link, page 95) or the Pentecost chapter from *A Year of Christian Festivals (Festival Time)* by Rita Storey (Franklin Watts, 2008) or *Christian Festivals* by Honor Head (Hachette, 2012).

Workshop 2/3A (Curriculum link: Literacy)

Take the story on from the point in time shown in the painting, or write about what might have led up to it for one of the groups of characters, such as the disciples or the onlookers.

Alternatively, begin or continue the writing (from Workshop 1) from the point of view of one of the characters (for example, 'If I were Peter…'). Write in the first person as if you were describing events as they happened, and ensure that you talk about thoughts and feelings as well as events.

Workshop 2/3B (Curriculum link: Literacy, Thinking and questioning)

Retell the story using figures and reflective storytelling (see *Godly Play Volume 4* or *The Big Story*). Encourage the children to generate their own 'I wonder' questions, especially about what the future would hold for the disciples. Write them on pieces of coloured paper or sticky notes and make a wall of questions about how Jesus' teachings and their experiences with Jesus would have prepared the disciples for the future.

Workshop 2/3C (Curriculum link: Art, History, Geography, DT)

Modernise the painting. It is worth knowing that Peter's preaching almost certainly occurred in the temple precincts, which could have held the large numbers of people mentioned in the story. Where would a similar event be held now? (The launch for the 2012 London Olympics took place in Trafalgar Square: how does that compare? Think about the similarities and differences, the impact of new technology, and so on.) Children could also find out about the upper room where the first events of Pentecost are said to have happened.

Alternatively, magnify one section of the painting, or divide the painting into sections, enlarging each section to make one very large class version. One class or group could imagine the scene at the beginning of the story in the upper room and another could look at the scene in the temple precinct.

Another option is to look at the whole Linaiuoli Triptych by Fra Angelico. If you wanted to make a modern version of the triptych showing the birth of the church at Pentecost, what would you put in each panel? Different groups could make the panels and then assemble them together.

Workshop 2/3D (Curriculum link: DT, History, Numeracy)

Make 3D models of the upper room or the temple precinct, and people to represent the disciples and the crowd. Use research to make sure that your models are accurate and in proportion and to find out where people may have come from, around the Mediterranean area.

Workshop 2/3E (Curriculum link: Drama, Thinking skills)

Either hot-seat characters from the painting or use a conscience alley activity to explore various aspects of the story: for example, should the disciples stay hidden in the upper room or go out and speak in the temple precinct? Should one of the visitors to Jerusalem believe the disciples?

As a class, discuss some of the thoughts that might have gone through the chosen characters' heads as they decided what to do. Encourage the children to think deeply about this and use their knowledge of the story.

Alternatively, debate the same questions or use PMI to discuss the questions.

Choices for Foundation Stage

- Read the story from *The Big Bible Storybook*.
- Dress up as the characters and act out the story.
- Tell the story with puppets or Playmobil™/small world characters.
- Make printed flames, windmills, kites, and so on.
- Retell the story by putting pictures in the right order.

Reflection for all Workshop 2/3 choices

Provide a laminated speech bubble, thought cloud and feeling heart shapes for each group. Older children or adults can scribe for younger children. Discuss and then write ideas about what one of the characters might say, what you think about the story or a character in it or its meaning, and how you or a character in the story feels.

'My Journey' reflection

On a small piece of paper, draw a picture or symbol to illustrate your Pentecost journey, and write the date next to it. Cut it out and stick it on to the timeline in your 'My Journey' book.

Generate an open or interesting question about the story and write it in the book. Alternatively, children could answer the following question in their book: What is the key moment of the story, and why does it matter?

Use scribes if necessary—it is important that a copy of the child's thoughts is included in the book in order for them to see their journey. Children should share their thoughts with a partner.

Whole-school worship

Preparation

Bring artwork together and display as much as possible. If a version of the picture has been made from small sections, it will need to be reassembled. Along the front of the hall, have dark material draped along the floor and a bowl of flame and wind shapes.

On an IWB, show an image of your chosen painting. Play seasonal music such as 'Come, Creator Spirit' by Keith Duke.

Engagement

Say, 'Imagine that we could all go to that room now with all the disciples waiting, wondering what to do next. I wonder what you would see… what you would notice… what you would hear… what you would feel? Perhaps it would be the sound of the wind rushing through the room, or the looks on the disciples' faces or being there in the crowd as they all hear the good news in whatever language they speak.'

Play some quiet music while two children from each class (more if appropriate or if time allows) walk to the front, take a flame shape or wind shape from the bowl and sprinkle it on the dark material, transforming its appearance.

As we see the dark material transformed and changed by the flames and wind shapes, we think about how the disciples were transformed and changed on the day of Pentecost, how we might be transformed and changed, and how we can transform and change the lives of others.

Suggested song

Sing a suitable song that the children know or have been taught for the day, such as 'Come, O Holy Spirit, Come', with both Nigerian and English words by John Bell and Alison Adam, which can be purchased as an mp3 download.

A child from each class can bring an example of work done during the workshops and share it with the rest of the school, saying why it is important or special for the Pentecost story.

Prayer

Use prayers written by the children in their workshops or from *The Lion Book of 1000 Prayers for Children* (pages 926–928).

Say, 'We are going to have a time when we will give thanks for the things we've enjoyed today. What would we like to say "thank you" for?' As suggestions are made, adults write them on flame shapes and the children place them on the dark material.

Say a prayer of thanks for 'all that we've been able to do and share together'.

Blessing

May God's Holy Spirit be in your life
 (hand on heart)
May God's Holy Spirit be in our world
 (sweep hand out in front)
May God's Holy Spirit be love between us
 (hold or shake hands)
And the blessing of God Almighty, Father, Son and Holy Spirit, be among us and remain with us this day and always. Amen

REVD DR SANDRA MILLAR

Unit 7 extension material

Class collective worship

Show a picture of wind and fire and ask, 'I wonder how this links to the journey day we enjoyed?' Show the picture or pictures used as a focus on the day. Give children the opportunity to revisit the story, generate questions and ideas from the journey day and add thoughts, questions or responses to their journal.

Reflection

Give each child the choice of a cut-out wind or fire shape, then ask them to hold it and think about how it inspired the disciples to go out and tell the good news to hundreds and thousands of people. Ask wondering questions:

- I wonder what gives you the strength to do new things?
- I wonder who you share good news with?
- I wonder if sharing good news makes both the sharer and the listener feel better?

Response

Play some quiet reflective music, such as the Taizé music recommended for the whole-school worship. Write on your wind or fire shape some good news you'd like to share. Peg the shapes to a string that can flutter in the breeze from a window or outside in a reflective garden if you have one at your school.

Prayer

Choose a prayer from *The Lion Book of 1000 Prayers for Children* (pages 926–928) or similar book.

Looking back on the journey

Plan a time of reflection on the theme for staff, governors and church visitors. Share and think about the story of someone who has continued in the footsteps of the apostles after the birthday of the church. It could be a famous Christian or someone you have met personally.

Reflect on some of the experiences from the journey day itself, or any follow-up work that has occurred within school or church.

Response

Look at the symbols of Pentecost: wind, fire, dove and so on. The feast of Pentecost offers Christians a chance to reflect on what the Holy Spirit brings to their lives. Reflect on what happens next in your journey as an individual or as a community, which of those gifts you can see in yourself and how they could help you on your journey.

Conclude the reflection with a time of silence, followed by a blessing:

May God's Holy Spirit be in your life
  (hand on heart)
May God's Holy Spirit be in our world
  (sweep hand out in front)
May God's Holy Spirit be love between us
  (hold or shake hands)
And the blessing of God Almighty, Father, Son and Holy Spirit, be among us and remain with us this day and always. Amen

REVD DR SANDRA MILLAR

Unit 7 church-based activity day

This can be a full day, half day or after-school club session.

Setting the scene

This session uses kites as a tool to explore the meaning of Pentecost. As a focal point, display different kites and pictures of them flying, or bring all the things you will need to make kites—string, reel, bamboo canes, paper or plastic (be careful with sheets of plastic if young children are present)—and ask an 'I wonder' question about what they might be for.

Display a Bible timeline, such as *The Big Bible Storybook Timeline*. If you have media facilities, you could show pictures or videos of kites accompanied by music.

Engagement

Fly a kite and/or show a video of a kite flying. Then ask, 'I wonder how flying a kite could help us celebrate Pentecost?'

Suggested activities

Provide some practical activities and some with aspects of research about kites. The research might involve websites or books. (If you can't access the internet at your location, print off appropriate material beforehand.) For suitable websites, see the web links on page 96.

- Find out how kite flying is linked to religious festivals—for example, the International Kite Festival held at Ahmedabad to celebrate Uttarayan, or Makar Sankranti at the end of winter.
- On a long thin piece of paper, draw a kite with a long tail and string. Write a poem about reaching up to God, and the themes of Pentecost. Write it so that the words go up into the sky like a kite, starting from the bottom, where someone is holding the string, and reaching right up into the sky where the kite is flying.
- Design, make and decorate a kite to show the message of Pentecost. Choose age-appropriate designs, as you want them to be flown at the end of the session and the next day after church.
- Design an altar frontal or banner using the kite theme and seasonal colours (red) for the all-age service.
- Show some prayer flags and explain that Tibetans believe that their prayers are carried on the wind. Read some Pentecost prayers—for example, from *The Lion Book of 1000 Prayers for Children* (pages 926–928). Children can write their own prayers and put them on kite or bunting shapes that can be hung or pegged on to string across the room.
- Make crowns with flame shapes around the top, to be worn for the worship later. Talk about what happened at the first Pentecost.
- Prepare food from around the Mediterranean to serve with pitta breads for the sharing time (to represent people from different places at the first Pentecost) or make iced kite-shaped biscuits (using diamond cookie cutters) for sharing later.

To get the most out of each activity, have a facilitator who can ensure that everyone thinks and talks about the meaning of Pentecost and what ideas and symbols to use in their designs.

Make or bring and share Mediterranean food together. Say the following grace with actions:

God bless us (hands on head)
God bless the food (hands around plate)
Amen (hands clasped together)

Worship

Read the story of Pentecost from a suitable Bible that will appeal to all ages (see page 11). *Children of God Storybook* by Desmond Tutu is a Bible written for children in Africa, highlighting the message of Pentecost that everyone hears the message wherever they live in the world.

Sing 'Wind and Fire' by Carolyn Warvel, to the tune of Frère Jacques:

Tongues of fire, Tongues of fire,
Mighty wind, Mighty wind,
The Holy Spirit's coming, The Holy Spirit's coming,
Praise the Lord! Praise the Lord!

UNIT 8

Following in Jesus' footsteps

Bible focus

Luke 5:1–11

Programme for the day

9.00–9.30am	Whole-school introduction to the day
9.30–10.35am	Workshop 1
10.35–10.55am	Break
10.55–12.00	Workshop 2
12.00–1.00pm	Lunch
1.00–1.15pm (or next day)	'My Journey' reflection
1.15–2.20pm	Workshop 3
2.20–2.30pm	Break
2.30–3.00pm	Whole-school worship

Preparation

Plan a time of reflection on the theme for governors, staff and church visitors.

Explain that Celtic knots first appeared around AD450 and were drawn to symbolise deep truths about God and life. The patterns have no end, to symbolise that God has no end. Many of the designs show that everything is part of one interwoven life, and are a means to explore the mystery and pattern of life that we can often only see when we stand back and reflect.

Invite each person to take a picture of a Celtic knot (available from the internet) and write in the pathways key moments, times and people on their life journey. Conclude the reflection with a time of silence or Celtic music played quietly—for example, 'Perfect Time' or 'The Love of God' by Maire Brennan, or *Celtic Roots and Rhythms* by Nick and Anita Haigh, or *Life Journey* CD by David Fitzgerald and Dave Bainbridge (Lindisfarne Scriptorium).

Look at your design. What do you notice? Does anything surprise you? Can you see links? Give thanks for the pattern of your life.

Bible reading

This is what the Lord says: 'Stand at the crossroads and look; ask for the ancient paths, ask where the good way is, and walk in it, and you will find rest for your souls.'

JEREMIAH 6:16 (NIV)

Whether you turn to the right or to the left, your ears will hear a voice behind you, saying, 'This is the way; walk in it.'

ISAIAH 30:21 (NIV)

Blessing

*You are the peace of all things calm,
You are the place to hide from harm
You are the light that shines in dark,
You are the heart's eternal spark
You are the door that's open wide,
You are the guest who waits inside
You are the stranger at the door,
You are the calling of the poor
You are my Lord and with me still,
You are my love, keep me from ill
You are the light, the truth, the way,
You are my Saviour this very day.*

TRADITIONAL CELTIC, FIRST CENTURY

Whole-school introduction to the day

Setting the scene

To explore the setting of the story through the senses, show images on a display or IWB—a lake, or footprints on the shore. Play Celtic music, such as songs by Moya Brennan or the hymn 'Be thou my vision'.

Share the story 'The footprints: Jesus chooses his first disciples' from *Bible Storybags* or read the story of the calling of the disciples from a suitable Bible. Talk about how people have been called by Jesus through the ages up to the present day. Perhaps children could have heard the *Bible Storybags* story read the day before in class and have already explored the wondering questions.

On an IWB, show a picture of Christians in church and ask, 'I wonder how this picture links with the story we have just heard?' Explain that you are going to explore how many people have followed in Jesus' footsteps over the last 2000 years.

Prayers

Show pictures from the Lindisfarne Scriptorium (see web link, page 96) or a Celtic cross.

Use parts of Morning Prayer from the Northumbria Community, the Iona Community or Church of England *Common Worship*, including the blessing at the end. Explain that these are daily prayers said by Christians all around the world (see web links, page 96).

Explain that everyone will come back together at the end of the day to share what they have found out about following in Jesus' footsteps.

Play the same music as the children go out to their workshops.

Use any of the above materials to make a reflection corner (see the *Pause for Reflection* pack for ideas).

Workshop 1: Be creative

Workshop 1A (Curriculum link: Music)

Learning intention

Children listen to a version of a Christian hymn expressing the belief that God is active in history. They reflect on the significance of the words for Christians.

Engagement

Play children the worship song 'Jesus, lover of my soul (It's all about you)' by Paul Oakley. Write the line 'No one else in history is like you, and history itself belongs to you' on the IWB.

Discuss what this might mean for Christians. Ask, 'I wonder how these words might encourage a Christian believer? I wonder how they might make a difference to the way they live their lives?'

Response

Tell the children that a number of hymns have been written to help Christians celebrate the lives of other believers through the centuries and to express the belief that God is always active in history.

Divide the children into three groups to explore different hymns. In their groups, ask them to listen to one of these hymns and look at the words.

- Lord, for the years
- For all the saints
- To be a pilgrim

Ask, 'I wonder what the main message of this hymn is? I wonder what questions you have? What imagery has the writer used?'

You could sing a hymn, with different groups or individuals leading a verse each. Children could compose percussion to accompany the verses.

Explain that hymn lyric writers and tune writers often work separately. Lyric writers may even write new words for old tunes. Ask the children to write their own hymn about walking in the footsteps of Jesus, setting the words to a familiar tune.

Reflection

Ask pupils to sit in a circle. In groups, tell the story of the hymn you have studied and the questions it raises for you. Children could teach one another the hymns or verses they have written.

Workshop 1B (Curriculum link: Drama)

Learning intention

Children learn about the life of Paul and the different journeys he undertook in order to spread the Christian faith. They reflect on the impact of Paul's journeys and preaching.

Engagement

Listen to the story of Saul's conversion on the road to Damascus. Talk to the children about how Saul's life was transformed from that day onwards, how he changed his name to Paul, and how he became an apostle who travelled and established new churches throughout the Roman Empire.

Show children a map of Paul's journeys on the IWB and talk about where he established new churches.

Response

Set the children the task of planning a documentary/drama about the journeys of Paul, with their joys and challenges. The 'docudrama' needs to conclude with an assessment of the impact of Paul's life on the Christian church. The children should create a storyboard to show the key events and, if time allows, create short drama extracts to illustrate them.

Reflection

Show or talk about the part of the docudrama that the children think is the most important or that they are most pleased with. Suggest one way in which Paul's life has made an impact on Christians today.

Workshop 1C (Curriculum link: Art)

Learning intention

Children reflect on the Christian value of *koinonia* ('community'). They then consider present-day Christian communities and what they can learn from them that might help them in their own lives.

Engagement

Display the word *koinonia* on the IWB, with pictures (such as a circle of friends, people at a meal, talking and listening, a parent playing with a child, someone caring for someone) that represent what it is, and ask the children to suggest what it might mean. Then write the word 'community' on the IWB. Ask, 'I wonder what this means?' Look at some definitions in the Oxford online dictionary.

Tell the children that the first Christians started as a small group of disciples but quickly grew into a large community that spread out over the Roman Empire. Read from Acts 2:43–47 (NCV):

The apostles were doing many miracles and signs, and everyone felt great respect for God. All the believers were together and shared everything. They would sell their land and the things they owned and then divide the money and give it to anyone who needed it. The believers met together in the Temple every day. They ate together in their homes, happy to share their food with joyful hearts. They praised God and were liked by all the people. Every day the Lord added those who were being saved to the group of believers.

What can we say were the key features of the early Christian community from this reading?

Listen to the song 'Christ be our light'. Ask, 'I wonder how this song mirrors the themes in the reading from Acts 2?'

Response

Throughout history, some Christians have chosen to live together in communities, while others have been part of a church community together with their own families. Some Christians still choose to live together in communities today, following a common pattern of life and prayer. Find out about modern-day communities from the web links on page 96.

Design a logo for one of these communities, with a title banner for the homepage of the website. You will need to represent the purpose, values, promises and commitment that underpin the Christian community.

Reflection

Share your designs. Notice similarities and differences, and produce visual representations, such as mind maps or Venn diagrams, of what they all have in common and which aspects are unique. Ask 'I wonder what you can learn from these communities that might help you in your own life?'

Workshop 1D (Curriculum link: Drama and dance)

Learning intention

Children learn how Paul wrote to the early church communities around the Mediterranean region in order to share important teaching about the Christian faith. Pupils reflect on Paul's writing about the Christian concept of love and consider the significance of each aspect of love described.

Engagement

The apostle Paul wrote letters to the early church communities situated around the Mediterranean in order to share important teaching about the Christian faith. These letters are in the New Testament and are still used by Christians today.

Read one or both of the following passages about love from Paul's letters: Romans 12:9–21 and 1 Corinthians 13.

Response

In groups, create a dance or drama about one of the qualities of love in action as described in the Bible reading(s). Children could use words and music in this activity. It would be helpful to have the reading(s) on display.

Reflection

Share your dances or dramas according to the order in which the qualities appear in the reading, and evaluate them with two stars and a wish. Ask, 'I wonder if one of the aspects of love in the reading(s) is more important than the others, or whether you can't have one without the others?'

Workshop 1E (Curriculum link: Art)

Learning intention

Children learn about the Christian belief in Jesus as the 'light of the world' and the call to his followers to be lights in the world today.

Engagement

On a table, place candles of different sizes, shapes and designs. Reflect on the fact that they all give out light. We too are all different but we still have the capacity to be a light shining in the world. The Bible calls Jesus 'the light of the world'. Christians believe that we are called to be lights of the world and follow Jesus' example.

Response

Draw a design for a candle holder, or make a clay candle holder, or decorate a candle with Christian symbols.

Reflection

Light a candle and put it where everyone can see it. Reflect on how you could be a light in the world. You could draw or write your ideas on an individual or class candle shape.

Workshop 1F (Curriculum link: Art)

Learning intention

Children look at the work of monks in the scriptoria, as well as modern-day calligraphers, to see how decoration can enhance the written word. They complete a piece of calligraphy based on a well-known Bible passage and are able to talk about their choice of words and design and its significance.

Engagement

Provide a tray with quills, a cuttlefish bone, scallop shells, gold foil (to look like gold leaf), paint, ink and parchment. Alternatively, show pictures of these items on the IWB. Ask, 'I wonder who would use these tools, and what they would be used for?'

Explain that these are the tools that monks would have used to copy the Bible, important scriptures and stories of saints. Show a picture of monks working in a scriptorium and talk about why it was such important work. Ask, 'I wonder why they made such complicated designs?'

Look at Christian Celtic design and, in particular, the work of monks producing illuminated texts using calligraphy, such as the Lindisfarne Gospels (see web link on page 96) or The Book of Kells. Focus on one or two Celtic Christian symbols—for example, the Trinity.

Show modern examples of Celtic design (see web links, page 96)—for example, from the Lindisfarne Scriptorium, Tess Cooling's work, or the work of Sue Symon, whose masterpiece *One Man's Journey to Heaven*, also known as the Bath Abbey Diptych, is an awe-inspiring work of art and craft. The life of Christ is depicted in 35 pairs of sumptuously decorated panels in a combination of needlework, hand-drawn lettering, illumination and calligraphy.

Ask, 'I wonder why they decorate the texts? I wonder what it adds to the text?'

Response

Display the following biblical texts about following in Jesus' footsteps: John 15:12, Galatians 5:22–23, or selected verses from Psalm 23 or 1 Corinthians 13.

Using calligraphy pens if available, copy a text from the Bible and decorate it using gold and silver pens. Colour with watercolour pencils and then wash over with water. For this activity, it is best to choose a short text.

Reflection

Show your calligraphy to a response partner. Talk about why you chose a particular Bible verse and how you have used colour and design to enhance the text.

Workshop 1G (Curriculum link: Art, Science)

Learning intention

Children look at the way images and inspiring photographs of nature can enhance prayer. They take their own photos and create a prayer card.

Engagement

Show a PowerPoint presentation that uses amazing images from nature. Look at prayer cards that use photos and some that don't. Ask wondering questions:

- I wonder how these might help a Christian to pray or reflect?
- I wonder if the natural world inspires people to pray?
- I wonder what would inspire you to pray?

Response

Provide a bank of suitable prayers or ask the children to write their own. Provide each child with an A6 or postcard-sized piece of card.

Take photos in the school grounds, download them on to the computer, and either make two prints to stick on to an A5 or A6 card so that the children can write their prayer on top of the picture, or create your own reflection card on the computer by superimposing the words of the prayer on top of the photo, printing off two copies (one to keep and one to give away). It may be more practical for an adult to print these afterwards.

Reflection

Think about how you could use your reflection card to help you have a quiet thinking time or a time to pray. Think about who you would like to give your second reflection card to, and why it might be helpful for them.

Workshop 1H
(Curriculum link: Art, History, Geography)

Learning intention

Children learn about the importance of the cross as a symbol for Christians throughout the world, representing the death of Christ on the cross. They learn that different styles reflect cultures around the world and have symbolic meaning. They design a cross for themselves, their school or a Christian.

Engagement

Show a simple wooden cross, or a picture of one, and ask the children what it symbolises.

The cross is a central symbol for Christians throughout the world. Explain that some are very simple, like the one you've just looked at, but that there are hundreds of designs, some of which are very complex. Many of these designs reflect the culture of the place where they are situated.

Look at the symbolism of three or four crosses from around the world as a way of showing how the designs, or the way they are used, help Christians now to follow Jesus' teaching. You can see many different crosses in *A-Cross the World* by Martyn Payne and Betty Pedley, a downloadable book from www.barnabasinschools.org.uk, or find out about them on the internet or from your local church. It is easy to find pictures of El Salvadoran picture crosses (for example, the story of Marie Gomez, 'Christ in the Community' from McCrimmons). You could also look at the work of the wood sculptor Jonathon Hemingray (see web links, page 96).

Response

Design your own cross, either one for yourself that shows what matters to you or what inspires you in your life, or one for your school, or one for a Christian. You will need to be able to explain what your design means, shows or symbolises.

Reflection

Put the designs up on a board or display and walk around the 'gallery' while quiet music plays. In pairs or small groups, share which ones you liked or found helpful, and why.

Workshop 2: Be communicative

Workshop 2A (Curriculum link: Thinking and questioning)

Learning intention

Children learn that the New Testament contains letters written to Christian communities and churches to help them understand the significance of Jesus and his teachings. They consider how today's communication methods might affect the ability of people to share that news in future.

Engagement

Brainstorm all the ways you could send someone a message if you wanted to share some amazing news. Show the children lots of examples from the letters in the New Testament. Explain who wrote these letters and why. You could show the following film clip explanation from the BBC learning zone (see web link, page 96).

Response

Propose this question to be discussed: you are a Christian who wants to tell a group of people the good news about Jesus' life and what he says. Is it better to write a letter or an email or to use another modern method of communication?

In groups, use PMI to sort out your ideas, allowing exactly five minutes for each section. After each section, share responses from each group with the whole class.

Reflection

As a class, decide which is better—writing a traditional letter or using a modern method—and why. Think about how we keep information now, and what effect temporary unrecorded means of communication might have on future generations.

Workshop 2B (Curriculum link: Art)

Learning intention

Children explore the Bible passage about love written by Paul and reflect on the meaning of the words for them.

Engagement

Read 1 Corinthians 13:4–7. Then re-read it, replacing the word 'love' with the word 'I'. Generate thoughts and questions in response to the passage; write them on sticky notes, and make a wall display or create a page on the IWB. Ask, 'I wonder what this tells us about being a Christian? I wonder how replacing "love" with "I" changes the meaning of the words for you?'

Response

Create a storyboard, PowerPoint presentation or piece of art that communicates the ideas about Christian love in this passage.

Reflection

Play some music on the theme of love while the children take some time to go round and look at the different ideas produced.

Workshop 2C (Curriculum link: Literacy)

Learning intention

Children learn about the structure of the letters in the Testament written by Paul. After looking at a Bible passage and/or a hymn about encouragement, they express their own ideas about this theme.

Engagement

Explain that Paul travelled round the Mediterranean area, preaching about Jesus and Christianity, shortly after Jesus' death. He could not stay in one place for very long, so he wrote letters to give the Christian communities and churches advice and guidance. Some of these letters are now to be found in the New Testament.

The basic format of Paul's letters is common to all letter writers in his day, using a form and style that the readers at the time would have recognised. It consists of:

- an opening salutation that mentioned the sender and the recipient, and then gave a greeting.
- a word of thanksgiving.
- the main body of the letter.
- a closing remark.

Paul wrote in one of his letters, 'Speak to one another with psalms, hymns and spiritual songs. Sing and make music in your heart to the Lord, always giving thanks to God the Father for everything, in the name of our Lord Jesus Christ' (Ephesians 5:19–20, NIV).

Christians are still encouraged by psalms, hymns and spiritual songs today. Listen to or look at the words of 'Lord, for the years' by Timothy Dudley-Smith. You can read about what inspired him at the web link on page 96.

Response

Either write your own letter of encouragement to a church today, following the format used by Paul, or write a verse for a hymn, song or poem of encouragement for the church today, based on 'Lord, for the years'.

Reflection

Share your best line with the class.

Workshop 2D (Curriculum link: Literacy, Drama)

Learning intention

Children explore how Christians in the past have been inspired to follow in Jesus' footsteps and how these people's lives can inspire Christians today. They reflect on whether these stories also inspire them.

Engagement

Show the justice pages from The Hub, a Christian website (see web link, page 96). These pages show how young Christians today can be inspired to make a difference, by the response of Christians to similar problems in Victorian times and by the words and actions of Jesus himself.

Response

Give each group some information about a famous Christian who is remembered because of their Christian actions (see web link, page 96).

Act out one of the scenarios from the past, showing how people were inspired by Jesus' actions and by their Christian faith to act in a certain way.

Reflection

Watch the performances and reflect on how they might inspire Christians and others now, helping people to understand Jesus' teachings. Ask, 'I wonder if it inspires you too?'

Workshop 2E (Curriculum link: Thinking and questioning)

Learning intention

Children consider the Christian belief that God is in all things and think about how that would affect their lives. They look at the Christian creed and consider how Christians communicate what they believe in. They then reflect on their own beliefs.

Engagement

Look at the pages from the Christian website The Hub that talk about the Christian creed (see web link, page 96).

Response

In twos or threes, take a line from the creed and produce your own PowerPoint slide or poster to explain and expand on the ideas in that part of the creed.

Reflection

Ask, 'I wonder what you believe about God, the world, and your own place in it?'

Workshop 2F (Curriculum link: Literacy)

Learning intentions

Children look at how Christians use prayers written by others. They write their own, using the style of specific Celtic prayers or hymns as a template.

Engagement

Talk about what prayer is, or watch the explanation on the BBC learning zone (see web link, page 96). Ask, 'I wonder why people like, or find it helpful to read or use, prayers written by others?'

Read one or more traditional Celtic prayers, or modern prayers written in a Celtic style, such as the following.

You are the peace of all things calm,
You are the place to hide from harm
You are the light that shines in dark,
You are the heart's eternal spark
You are the door that's open wide,
You are the guest who waits inside
You are the stranger at the door,
You are the calling of the poor
You are my Lord and with me still,
You are my love, keep me from ill
You are the light, the truth, the way,
You are my Saviour this very day.

TRADITIONAL CELTIC, FIRST CENTURY

May the road rise up to meet you.
May the wind be always at your back.
May the sun shine warm upon your face;
May the rains fall soft upon your fields
and until we meet again,
may God hold you in the palm of his hand.

TRADITIONAL GAELIC BLESSING

Deep peace of the running wave to you.
Deep peace of the flowing air to you.
Deep peace of the quiet earth to you.
Deep peace of the shining stars to you.
Deep peace of the son of peace to you.

TRADITIONAL CELTIC BLESSING

Ask, 'I wonder what you notice about what these prayer writers have written about?' Talk about Celtic Christianity, with its themes of presence (of God), protection (by God) and pilgrimage (life's journey). Information can be found at the web links on page 96.

Response

Provide a Celtic pattern-edged writing frame. Write your own prayer in the Celtic style, using one of the above prayers as a template.

Reflection

Sit outside, perhaps in your school's reflective garden, or light candles and share some of the prayers and blessings.

Workshop 3: Be knowledgeable

Workshop 3A (Curriculum link: History, Geography)

Learning intention

Children investigate how the early church started and spread, and reflect on how Christians today feel about being part of a long line of Christians through history.

Engagement

Recap the *Bible Storybags* story 'The footprints' from the beginning of the day. Recall the last lines: 'The five becomes twelve… the twelve becomes a hundred… the hundred becomes a thousand… the thousand becomes a million… the million becomes billions.'

Explain that Christianity is the largest religion in the world. Connect to 'Jump into a picture: Pentecost' if you have explored that journey day in your school, explaining that Pentecost was the birthday of the church. The disciples then spread out to take the good news around the Mediterranean region.

Response

In groups, look at different ways in which good news spreads.

Research when Christianity arrived in India, Iraq, Iran, China, South America, Africa and Egypt, and who took it to these places (see the web links, page 96).

Add the information you have found out on to a class world map.

Reflection

Ask, 'I wonder what surprised you about what you have found out? I wonder how you feel about the fact that Christianity started in one place and is now all over the world? I wonder how people spread the good news of the Christian message today?'

Workshop 3B
(Curriculum link: History, Geography)

Learning intention

Children investigate Christianity's arrival in Britain, looking at who brought it, when and where, and recognise that Christianity has a long and important place in the history of our country.

Engagement

Show a Celtic timeline (see web links, page 96).

Show information about individual Celtic saints, such as Columba of Iona, Aidan of Lindisfarne or Augustine of Canterbury. For example, the following table shows key events during the life of Augustine of Canterbury.

Year	Event
560	Ethelbert becomes king of Kent and overlord of the surrounding kingdoms.
585	Gregory sees Angle slaves in Rome and dreams of converting them to Christianity.
590	Gregory the Great is elected pope.
596	Augustine and his monks arrive in Kent.
596	Monks are allowed to rebuild the church in Canterbury.
596	Ethelbert himself is baptised.
597	Ten thousand Saxons are baptised on Christmas Day.
603	Augustine attempts but fails to bring the Celtic church into communion with Rome.
604	Augustine dies.
660	Celtic and Roman churches are finally united.

Response

Create an individual or class annotated timeline for the arrival of Christianity, adding facts and thoughts, feelings and questions about what you have found out.

Reflection

Ask, 'I wonder what surprised you about the arrival of Christianity in Britain?'

Show a photo of very worn steps in an old church (Saxon churches are the oldest examples still in use in this country) and talk about or reflect on the faith of all the thousands of Christians who must have entered to worship and pray in that place. Write a response or feeling on a stone or a cut-out paper pebble shape.

Workshop 3C
(Curriculum link: History, Geography)

Learning intention

Chidren investigate Christianity in their locality to understand how the values held by Christians affect those people's lives. They reflect on the impact of the church on the local community and reflect on their own values.

Engagement

Show all your local churches on a map on the whiteboard.

Response

In groups, generate questions that you would like to ask Christians now. Interview the visitors from your local church, asking them your questions. Look at the REQuest website for ideas about the sort of questions you might ask (see web links, page 96).

Reflection

Ask, 'I wonder what difference it makes to people in your area to be a Christian? I wonder how it affects the way they contribute to the community? I wonder which values are important to Christians? I wonder which values you share with Christians?'

Workshop 3D
(Curriculum link: Geography)

Learning intention

Children explore the idea of pilgrimage and its value to Christians. They look at evidence of pilgrimage to sites in the UK.

Engagement

Show the film clip about Christian pilgrimage from the REQuest website. Then look at the different places of pilgrimage mentioned in the lesson plan and do the activity suggested there: 'Ask the children to think of five words to describe each of the images and three questions they would like to ask about each one' (see web links, page 96). Show pictures from Iona, Lindisfarne or Walsingham, which are all pilgrimage places in this country. Detailed information and resources about individual places of pilgrimage can be found on their websites.

Response

Identify the features of a pilgrimage and decide how it is different from an ordinary journey or trip. Design a pilgrimage in your area.

Reflection

As a way of reflecting on what they have found out about pilgrimage, the children should diamond-sort the statements about pilgrimage found on the REQuest website, about why a Christian might go on pilgrimage or what they themselves might get from visiting a place of pilgrimage (see web link, page 96).

Workshop 3E (Curriculum link: History)

Learning intention

Children explore the story of the Taizé community to see why it was set up and what impact it has on Christians today.

Engagement

Darken the room before the children enter, and set up a bank of nightlights. Ask them to enter without speaking and just to think about their reactions and any questions they may have.

Listen to a clip of music from the Taizé website (see web link, page 96) or download from iTunes. Look at an image of Taizé worship and at the bank of nightlights. Ask the children for their feelings, reactions and questions about the experience.

Explain how Taizé was founded by Brother Roger as a reaction to World War II. He believed that, through people living in community with others from all around the world, God's vision of peace could become a reality.

Response

During a meeting in the Church of Reconciliation, Brother Alois said, 'It is just like a feast to see so many young adults on the hill, in all their diversity. It gives us the great hope that humanity at peace is possible.'

Throughout the year, many young people arrive at Taizé to take part in the celebrations (see web link, page 96). Using your experience as you came into the workshop and information from the Taizé website, write a leaflet to help young pilgrims who are thinking about a visit to Taizé. You will need to include information about meetings at Taizé, what happens there each day, where to stay, preparation and other aspects of a visit to the community (see web link, page 96.)

Reflection

Taizé music and prayer are used throughout the world in churches. Ask some wondering questions:

- I wonder why you think Taizé's influence has spread so far?
- I wonder if you would like to go to Taizé?
- I wonder what we could use from Taizé in our own worship here at school?

Workshop 3F
(Curriculum link: PSHE, Citizenship)

Learning intention

Children explore the story of the L'Arche community of able and disabled people living together, to see why it was set up and what impact it has on Christians today.

Engagement

Jean Vanier founded L'Arche in 1967 with Father Thomas Philippe in Trosly, France. He rented a small home and welcomed Raphael Simi and Phillip Seux, two men with a developmental disability who had been living in an institution, to live with him. Today there are over 135 L'Arche communities in 30 countries. Information can be found online (see web links, page 96).

Watch some short videos about volunteering and about the community (see web links, page 96). Explain to the children that they will see able-bodied and disabled people in the films.

Ask the children if they have questions or thoughts and feelings about the film that they'd like to share with a partner or with the class.

Many Christians believe that they are called to walk alongside people in their lives, just as Jesus walked alongside the disciples on the road to Emmaus and with the poor, hungry, ill and outcast during his life on earth.

Read the prayer of St Teresa of Avila that begins, 'Christ has no body now but yours'.

Response

Research information from the website and produce a poster for a fundraising event for a L'Arche community. You will need to think about how people can identify it easily, what you might do to fundraise, and why people should support the fundraising effort.

Alternatively, research information from the website and write a job advert for a Christian volunteer to work at a L'Arche community. You will need to think about how you explain what the community is, what the voluntary work entails, and why a Christian might feel called to work there.

Reflection

Share different aspects of what you have learned. Ask some wondering questions.

- I wonder if you would volunteer at somewhere like the L'Arche community?
- I wonder what we learn from something like the L'Arche community about Christian values and life?
- I wonder what we learn about our own values and life?

Workshop 3G (Curriculum link: History, PHSE, Citizenship)

Learning intention

Children find out about saints through the ages, people who have lived their lives following in Jesus's footsteps. They create an interview sheet for one person they have found out about and give possible answers to the questions.

Engagement

Tell the story 'Introduction to the Communion of Saints' from *Godly Play Volume 7* and share the wondering questions.

Response

Have tables set up with different stories from *Godly Play Volume 7*, which includes the following saints: Thomas Aquinas; Valentine; Patrick; Catherine of Siena; Julian of Norwich; Columba; Elizabeth of Portugal; Augustine of Hippo; Mother Teresa of Calcutta; Teresa of Avila; Margaret of Scotland; Nicholas, Bishop of Myra. If you have chosen to look at a local saint or St Brendan, provide tables with information, pictures, maps, figures and objects to represent their story about these saints and their lives.

In groups, the children will tell the story to each other and work through the wondering questions. Set out a choice of art materials so that the children can produce a creative response to the story they have heard.

Using what you have found out or felt about the famous Christian in the story, create an interview sheet with questions you would like to have asked them and possible answers they would have given.

Alternatively, provide fact cards, books or web pages about any of the following: Elizabeth Fry, William Wilberforce, St Ignatius, Jackie Pullinger, Gladys Aylward, John Wycliffe, Corrie Ten Boom, William Tyndale, Desmond Tutu and Oscar Romero.

Reflection

Children can take turns to share what they have found out about each person.

Ask, 'I wonder what we can learn from the story you looked at? Having shared the stories, I wonder if you are particularly inspired by one person's story?'

Foundation workshop choices

Engagement

Retell the *Bible Storybags* story 'The footprints (Jesus chooses his first disciples)', and talk about how other people have spread the story of Jesus in the 2000 years since then. Tell the story of one example, such as Columba or Gladys Aylward.

Any of the stories in *Godly Play Volume 7* would be suitable for Foundation Stage.

Response

Use any of the workshop choices above that are suitable to adapt for Foundation stage, with a rotation of the following activities.

- Sand or water trays: Using figures and blocks to represent buildings or places, boats and so on, act out the story of the Christian person. Talk with the church visitors about what being a disciple of Jesus means to them. Record the children's comments around the picture of a church (ideally their local church).
- Roleplay: Act out the story of the good Samaritan or the lost sheep to show how God uses stories to teach his disciples to care for other people.
- Use the wondering questions in *Godly Play Volume 7*.
- Allow the children to retell the Godly Play story themselves and provide various art materials to allow them a free choice of how to express the story.

Suitable story books to explore include:

- *Jesus' Friends* by Christina Goodings
- *The Story of Tabitha and Friends* by Marilyn Lashbrook
- *Blessings Everywhere* by Dandi Daley-Mackall
- *The Lost Sheep and the Scary Day* by Claire Henley
- *The Good Stranger* by Nick Butterworth
- *You Are Very Special* by Su Box
- *The Lost Sheep* by Lois Rock

'My Journey' reflection

On a small piece of paper, draw a picture or symbol to illustrate a journey studied in the workshop, and write the date next to it. Cut it out and stick it on to the timeline in the 'My Journey' book.

Generate an open or interesting question about the story and write it in the book, or answer the following question in their book: What is the key moment of the story, and why does it matter?

Use scribes if necessary—it is important that a copy of the child's thoughts is included in the book in order for them to see their journey.

Share your thoughts with a partner.

Whole-school worship

Preparation

Cut out stepping stone shapes and place them across the floor or on a display. Bring representative examples of work produced—art, questions, map, and so on—to share with the rest of the school. Talk about each one with the ambassadors who bring them up, then place them on the stepping stones or add them to the display to show how Christians have followed in Jesus' footsteps throughout history. We can walk across the stepping stones, learning from the disciples of Jesus. Place blank stepping stones at the end of the line and ask the children to stand on them. How can their lives set a good example for others in the future?

Reflection

Use parts of Evening Prayer from *Common Worship* or from the Northumbria Community (see web links, page 96).

Prayer

Use prayers written by the children if they have done so, or suitable prayers from *The Lion Book of Children's Prayers* (pages 502–504).

Suggested songs

Be thou my vision
Lord, for the years
For all the saints
To be a pilgrim
Christ be our light (downloadable from www.musicnotes.com)

Blessing of St Columba

Be at peace, and love each other. Follow the example of good people and God will comfort and help you, now and in the future. Amen

Unit 8 extension material

Class collective worship

Talk about how Christians are following in Jesus' footsteps and the footsteps of countless Christians through the ages. With older children, ask if they can think of any examples they have experienced or heard about since the journey day, where they could see that people were following in Jesus' footsteps because of the way they acted. Ask younger children to think about times when they or someone they know has been kind or helpful.

You could give children the opportunity to revisit the story, generate questions and ideas from the journey day and add thoughts, questions or responses to their 'My Journey' book.

If you have *Godly Play Volume 7*, tell one of the stories of the saints, or read about a modern-day saint.

Reflection

Ask the wondering questions in the Godly Play story, or the following questions:

- On the journey day, we had a line of stepping stones showing how Christians have followed Jesus through history. Can anyone remember who was on the last few stones? (Children)
- Since that journey day, we have each journeyed on through our lives to this point. Reflect back on all the people who have guided you and inspired you throughout the last few weeks.
- I wonder what these people did that was so special?
- I wonder how they showed they were following in Jesus' footsteps?
- I wonder if you could imagine following in Jesus' footsteps in the same way?

Response

Provide a template of a series of paper stepping stones and ask children to write or draw on each stone something or someone or an event that has helped them on their journey.

Alternatively, give each child one or two paper stepping stones to write on. When they are complete, add them to a stepping stone line right across the classroom.

Prayer

We thank you, God, for everyone who has inspired us as we journey through life. Amen

Blessing of St Columba

Be at peace, and love each other. Follow the example of good people and God will comfort and help you, now and in the future. Amen

Looking back on the journey

Plan a time of reflection on the theme for staff, governors and church visitors. Think about the story of someone who has lived the life of a pilgrim (for example, Brother Roger of Taizé), or listen to the story of someone who has been on a modern pilgrimage.

Reflect on some of the experiences from the journey day itself, or any follow-up work that has occurred within school or church. Think about yourself as part of God's unfolding story, and how we are all called to be disciples, pilgrims and saints.

Prayer

You are the peace of all things calm,
You are the place to hide from harm
You are the light that shines in dark,
You are the heart's eternal spark
You are the door that's open wide,
You are the guest who waits inside
You are the stranger at the door,
You are the calling of the poor
You are my Lord and with me still,
You are my love, keep me from ill
You are the light, the truth, the way,
You are my Saviour this very day.

TRADITIONAL CELTIC, FIRST CENTURY

Response

On squares of paper, write words from the reflection above (for example, light, peace, calm, love and truth) or other values or gifts that will support you on your journey. Fold each corner in to the middle. Float in a tray or bowl of shallow water.

Play quiet music or conclude the reflection with a time of silence followed by the blessing of St Columba:

Be at peace, and love each other. Follow the example of good people and God will comfort and help you, now and in the future. Amen

Unit 8 church-based activity day

This can be a full day, half day or after-school club session.

Setting the scene

Create a focal point on the theme of 'To be a pilgrim'. Display a hat, walking stick, large scallop shell on a red string, small backpack, cloak or waterproof, pilgrim badge symbols (for example, yellow arrows or scallop shells from Santiago). Display a Bible timeline such as *The Big Bible Storybook Timeline*, but extend the line to present times. If you have media facilities, you could show pictures of pilgrims from different eras, accompanied by music.

Welcome everyone and introduce the theme for the day. Point to the timeline and explain that we are all called to be pilgrims—disciples of Jesus. People over the centuries have gone on pilgrimage as a physical and spiritual way of thinking about the journey of their life, and still do so now. Many find it a deeply moving experience.

Story

Tell the following story of how John Bunyan wrote *Pilgrim's Progress*.

John Bunyan grew up in turbulent times. He was born in 1628 at Elstow, just south of Bedford. His father was a tinker who wandered around mending pots and pans for people. He converted to Christianity in 1653 during Cromwell's Protectorate and became a much-loved local preacher of the gospel. When Charles II came to the throne in 1660, preaching by dissenters was forbidden and Bunyan was thrown into prison for twelve years for disobeying this rule. He began writing *Pilgrim's Progress* while he was in prison. When he was released, he became a very famous preacher and church leader.

Pilgrim's Progress or, to give it its full title, *The Pilgrim's Progress from This World to That Which Is to Come*, is a allegory of the Christian journey and was published in 1678. The main character dreams of his journey to heaven, describing metaphors for all the challenges that he might face along the way. This book has been translated into more than 200 languages—more than any other book except the Bible.

Suggested activities

- Listen to the hymn 'To be a pilgrim' and think about what the words mean. Rewrite them in your own words. Each group could take one verse, or you could add a new verse.
- Draw a path or labyrinth on the floor, or mark one out with rope or tape. Put twists and turns in it. You could add challenges or ask the children and adults to think of challenges that we come across in our spiritual life. Walk down the path, thinking about how Christian felt. Draw your own life path or labyrinth so far and put symbols or markers where important or special things happened that are part of your journey. Add your hopes and dreams for the future. Ask yourself questions such as: What has happened in my life that has felt like twists and turns along an unknown path? Have there been times that felt like twists away from or towards God? You could choose to share your life story with a partner.
- Using what you know about John Bunyan and how he came to write *Pilgrim's Progress*, write a mini biography or introduction card about him. Alternatively, draw a person shape and add details about him to the picture. You could write or draw things in appropriate areas. For example, near his heart, write that he loved God or that he was courageous; draw a pen in his hand and write, 'He wrote about…'; in a speech bubble, write how he told people God loved them, and so on. You could draw a pen or book for him to carry, or draw other pictures round him to represent his life—for example, a prison cell.
- Make a banner or altar frontal based on *Pilgrim's Progress*, showing life as a journey. You could look at images such as the Pilgrims' Progress window at the Christian Reformed Church in Holland, Michigan (see web link, page 96).
- Talk about the burdens that Christian carries. Make (or prepare in advance) a pile of burdens by rolling up newspapers and wrapping them in plain paper. Using marker pens, write on the shape a burden that we might carry. See how many burdens you can pick up. Alternatively, work as a team to pile many burdens on one person's back, and then let all the burdens fall at the foot of the cross. Talk about how Jesus' death for us on the cross means

that we don't have to carry the burdens of sin; we are forgiven by grace.
- Make a mock prison with bars in a smallish space and sit inside. Talk about what it feels like. Tell that part of John Bunyan's story and discuss what he might have felt like and how he used the situation for God's glory.
- Show pilgrim badges or pictures of them. Ask, 'I wonder why you would want to wear a pilgrim badge? I wonder if you'd want to have it to wear during the pilgrimage or at the end, when you have completed it?' Once the children have wondered about these ideas, explain that the scallop shell is a worldwide symbol of pilgrimage because it is the symbol of St James, a saint who is buried at Santiago de Compostela in Spain. This was the second most important pilgrimage site, after Jerusalem, for hundreds of years and is very popular again today. There are a number of explanations of why the scallop shell became the symbol for this pilgrimage:
  - James (Jesus' brother) preached the gospel in that part of Spain. There is a story that, as James arrived there by boat, a bridegroom's horse panicked. The bridegroom fell into the sea, but, through a miracle, he emerged covered in shells and rode away.
  - The grooves on a scallop shell represent the routes to Compostela from all over Europe (as far away as Russia), merging at the shrine.
  - Just as the waves wash scallop shells to the shore, God's hand guides pilgrims to Compostela.
  - Pilgrims used scallop shells to pick up drinking water and to hold offerings of food, and so on.
  - These shells were common along the shore at Finisterre (meaning literally 'the end of the world') and pilgrims collected them to show that they had completed the pilgrimage.
- Design your own pilgrim badge to represent your local church or area or make a shell on a red string using cardboard, fimo or air-dried clay. You will need:
  - Badge sized pieces of cardboard or air-drying or fimo clay
  - Plastic craft mat and rolling pin
  - Tools (such as a plastic craft clay knife)
  - Thread or cord to wear the badge round your neck, or a badge pin to glue on the back

  To make a cardboard badge, cut out the shape and paint or colour the design on the front. Make two holes and thread with cord or glue a badge pin on the back.

  Alternatively, take a small amount of clay and work it with your hands to soften it up. Place the clay on the plastic craft mat and flatten it a little. Roll with a rolling pin until it is about 5mm thick. Cut out your chosen badge or shell shape and smooth the edges with your fingers. If it is to be worn round the neck, use a small stick to create a hole or two holes. Follow the instructions to set the clay and finally thread the cord through the holes or glue the pin on the back.
- Make a pilgrim's scrip or satchel. Decide what you would need to put in your bag as a pilgrim. Draw or write these items on cards and add them to your bag. Think about adding values and gifts that could help you on your journey—for example, knowing God loves you, inspiring people, experiences you've had, and so on.
- Arrange a short prayer walk round your church as a mini-pilgrimage. At the end, you could go and place a footprint at the spot that you feel represents where you are on your journey, or each person could carry a few footprints and leave one at each place to show that you prayed there.

Make or bring and share food together. Say or sing grace before eating.

Worship

Tell the story 'The footprints: Jesus chooses his first disciples' from *Bible Storybags*. Make the link between the disciples in Bible times, the disciples through the ages whom the children found out about at school, and the story of *Pilgrim's Progress* and the fact that we are all pilgrims on a journey.

Share some of the ideas or objects that have been created during the activities. You could choose to do the prayer walk as you worship together.

Suggested songs

Be thou my vision
Lord, for the years
For all the saints
To be a pilgrim
Christ be our light (downloadable from www.musicnotes.com)

Blessing of St Columba

Be at peace, and love each other. Follow the example of good people and God will comfort and help you, now and in the future. Amen

DOWNLOADABLE APPENDICES

Guidance sheet for volunteers

Thank you so much for volunteering to help with this exciting project. This journey day is valuable for both the church and school communities because:

- It builds links between church and school, enabling them to work and worship together and build good community relationships.
- It provides an opportunity for children to encounter and explore Bible stories and Christianity in a contemporary context.
- It provides opportunities for spiritual development for everyone involved, aiming to increase reflective skills and articulacy in spiritual language.
- It provides opportunities for learning outside the classroom.
- It supports RE-led integrated learning and enhances teaching and learning in RE, enabling children to learn about and from religion, and can act as a model for learning in the church context—for example, at holiday or activity clubs, in Sunday groups or worship.

Your role

The input from you as a church volunteer adds considerably to pupils' experience, providing a Christian faith viewpoint and knowledge. You can encourage questions and bring empathy to activities and learning. You also significantly improve the adult–child ratio, enabling more opportunities for listening and talking with children. This facilitates thinking and questioning, and builds relationships and understanding.

Ensure that you use open-ended and 'I wonder' questions, as these ensure that you do not limit pupils' responses to short answers or the answers that they think you are looking for. Rather, they enable children to offer creative and detailed answers.

You can add real value to the day by writing down some of the children's thoughts and ideas to share with staff.

Information sheets

Information Sheet 1: Volunteer helpers/groups		
Workshop		
Name of class or group	Name of class or group	Name of class or group
Volunteer names	Volunteer names	Volunteer names
'Floating'		

Information Sheet 2: Workshop information			
Location Leader Support staff	Workshop 1: Title/focus	Workshop 2: Title/focus	Workshop 3: Title/focus

Web links

Introduction

- www.godlyplay.org.uk (*Godly Play* books by Jerome Berryman)
- www.pipwilson.com (*Blob Spirituality*)
- http://gloucester.anglican.org/parish-life/jumping-fish (*Pause for Reflection* pack)

Unit 1

- http://gloucester.anglican.org/parish-life/jumping-fish (*Values for Life* disk)
- www.heqigallery.com (He Qi art)
- www.mccrimmons.com (creation art)
- http://Bibletimeline.info (Bible timeline)
- www.sermons4kids.com/powerpoint_presentations.htm
- www.interviewwithgod.com/faith (PowerPoint presentation about faith)

Unit 2

- www.tts-group.co.uk (search for 'Reflect a Story' and select 'Christian creation')
- www.nationalgallery.org.uk (search artist Seurat)
- https://hwb.wales.gov.uk. Enter the site, click on 'Find and use' and search 'pointillist paintings' (pointillism)
- www.calgaryartinnature.co.uk (natural materials used in art)
- www.goldsworthy.cc.gla.ac.uk (natural materials used in art: the work of Andy Goldsworthy)
- www.natre.org.uk/spiritedarts/art06/where_is_god/index.php (images of God in various media)
- www.mccrimmons.com ('Behold' poster/'Creation' banner)
- www.sophiehacker.com
- www.wellsprings.org.uk/liturgies/creation.htm (Wellspring Creation Liturgy)
- www.lindisfarne-scriptorium.co.uk (calligraphy examples)
- www.its.caltech.edu/~atomic/snowcrystals/photos/photos.htm (snowflake photos)
- www.keplersdiscovery.com/Proportion.html (snowflakes and individuality)
- www.keplersdiscovery.com/Proportion.html (Fibonacci sequence)
- www.mcs.surrey.ac.uk/Personal/R.Knott/Fibonacci/fibnat.html#petals (Fibonacci sequence)
- www.solarviews.com/eng/earthsp.htm (images of earth from space)
- http://nineplanets.org (Google Earth 'The Nine Planets')
- www.atelieryannarthusbertrand.com/en/11-collection ('Earth from above' photos by Yann Arthus-Bertrand)
- www.suepalmer.co.uk
- ew.ecocongregation.org/resources/module2 (eco-congregation resources)
- ew.ecocongregation.org (information on being an eco-congregation)

Unit 3

- www.rhematheatre.org/dvd (*Miracle Mysteries* DVD)
- www.muzu.tv or www.youtube.com (U2 'Walk on' video)
- www.childrenssociety.org.uk/news-views/our-blog/young-refugees-share-their-stories (stories about refugees)
- www.northumbriacommunity.org/pray-the-daily-office/complines (traditional night service)
- www.ehow.com/how_4487799_build-model-molecular-structure-diamond.html (model carbon molecules)
- www.windows2universe.org/citizen_science/starcount (worldwide star count)
- www.origami-fun.com/origami-stars.html (printed instructions)
- www.findmypast.co.uk/family-tree-explorer.jsp (family history website)
- www.bbc.co.uk (*Who Do You Think You Are?*)

Unit 4

- www.bridgemanart.com (search for 'Roger Wagner triptych') (*Triptych, 2000*)
- www.womeninthebible.net/paintings_ruth.htm (images and background information on the story of Ruth)

- http://winchester-cathedral.org.uk/cathedral/wp-content/uploads/Childrens-Trail-Leaflet.pdf (welcome leaflets)
- www.manchestercathedral.org/a-good-day-out/families-and-children (Explorer trail)
- www.bsuh.nhs.uk/patients-and-visitors/coming-into-hospital/monkey-goes-to-hospital-patient-information-leaflet-for-young-children (welcome leaflets)
- www.biblesociety.org.uk/products/9780564038862 (Testament: Bible in Animation DVDs)
- www.Bible-archaeology.info/work.htm (information on gleaning and family life in Bible times)
- www.visualbiblealive.com/stock_image.php?id=29725 (Ruth and Naomi's journey)
- www.womenintheBible.net/3.3.Clothing_housing.htm (family life in Bible times)
- www.womenintheBible.net/3.1.Family_Work_Religion.htm (family life in Bible times)
- www.brainboxx.co.uk/A3_ASPECTS/pages/TALKenvoy.htm (envoying technique)
- http://anamchara.com/mystics/julian (biography of Julian of Norwich)
- www.randomactsofkindness.org
- www.chpublishing.co.uk/books/9780715143148/love-life-live-lent-kids (includes more random acts of kindness)
- www.restore-uk.org (Birmingham Churches Together project)
- www.restore-uk.org/kidz (befriending scheme)
- www.childrenssociety.org.uk (information about refugees)
- www.christianaid.org.uk (work with refugees)
- www.cafod.org.uk (work with refugees)
- www.pauline-uk.org (Sieger Köder Easter paintings)
- www.joyfulheart.com/easter/tissot-passion.htm (James Tissot Easter paintings)
- www.bdeducation.org.uk/shop/last-supper-card-set-bdbe002ls.html (cards to accompany *Last Supper* poster)
- www.whyeaster.com (celebrations of Easter round the world)
- http://request.org.uk/festivals/easter (Easter resources)
- www.bbc.co.uk/learningzone/clips (the Easter story). Search in 'Religious Education', then 'Christianity: Celebrations and Festivals'
- www.bbc.co.uk/learningzone/clips/sophies-easter/3719.html ('Sophie's Easter')
- www.bbc.co.uk/learningzone/clips/the-eucharist-or-holy-communion/4458.html (three-minute film on Communion)
- http://request.org.uk/life/worship-life/communion-life/2013/07/08/communion (video on Communion)
- www.nottsopenchurches.org.uk/education-primary.php (KS1 resource on Communion: download PDF and refer to Section 2, 'At the Altar')
- www.bbc.co.uk/news/uk-13155573 (video clip of the Queen and Maundy money)
- www.projectbritain.com/easter/goodfriday.htm (Woodland Junior School)
- www.bbc.co.uk/learningzone/clips/the-crucifixion-and-peters-denial/677.html (Peter's denial)
- www.heqigallery.com/shop/46The-Road-to-Emmaus.jpg (*Road to Emmaus* painting by He Qi)
- www.nationalgallery.org.uk/paintings/altobello-melone-the-road-to-emmaus (*Road to Emmaus* painting by Melone)

Unit 5

- www.bbc.co.uk/learningzone/clips/the-first-christmas/7017.html ('The First Christmas')
- www.mind-mapping.co.uk (examples and explanations of mind mapping)

Unit 6

- www.bdeducation.org.uk/shop/communion-confirmation/last-supper-poster-bdbe001ls.html (*Last Supper* poster)
- www.nationalgallery.org.uk (classical paintings of the Easter story)
- www.joyfulheart.com/easter (includes modern paintings of the Easter story)

Unit 7

- www.pauline-uk.org/product.asp?ID=2139 (Turvey Abbey Pentecost Celebration poster)
- www.nationalgallery.org.uk/paintings/giotto-and-workshop-pentecost
- www.giottodibondone.org/Pentecost-1320-25.html
- www.giottodibondone.org/No.-39-Scenes-from-the-Life-of-Christ--23.-Pentecost-1304-06.html
- www.mccrimmons.com (*Way of Light* poster set: 'Pentecost' or *Power of the Spirit* poster: 'Pentecost' by Sr Sheila Gosney RJM)
- www.methodist.org.uk/static/artcollection/image34.htm (*Untitled—Pentecost* by John Brokenshire)
- www.sophiehacker.com (*Whirlwind and Wellspring*)
- http://request.org.uk/oldsite/unpacked/celebrations/pentecost/pentecost.htm (how Christians celebrate Pentecost)

- www.childrenschapel.org/Biblestories/pentecost.html (story of Pentecost)
- www.my-best-kite.com (research on kites)
- www.grc.nasa.gov/WWW/K-12/airplane/kite1.html (research on kites)
- www.my-best-kite.com/chinese-kites.html (a history of kite-making, including information on how they are used in festivals. There are records of kites being made in China for 3000 years.)

Unit 8

- www.lindisfarne-scriptorium.co.uk (Celtic art and *Life Journey* CD)
- www.northumbriacommunity.org/offices/morning-prayer (morning prayer)
- www.ionabooks.com/1189-PL10001-Morning-Service-Iona-Abbey.html (morning prayer)
- www.churchofengland.org/prayer-worship/worship/texts/principal-services/word/morning.aspx (morning prayer)
- www.hilfieldfriary.org.uk (modern-day communities)
- www.worthabbey.net (modern-day communities)
- www.ffald-y-brenin.org (modern-day communities)
- www.beunos.com (modern-day communities)
- www.taize.fr/en (modern-day communities)
- www.northumbriacommunity.org (modern-day communities)
- www.maybe.org.uk (modern-day communities)
- www.bl.uk/onlinegallery/sacredtexts/lindisfarne.html (Lindisfarne Gospels)
- www.lindisfarne-scriptorium.co.uk/gallery/art-prints-c-15.html (Celtic design)
- www.cooligraphy.co.uk (Celtic design by Tess Cooling)
- www.mccrimmons.com (*Christ in the Community* by Marie Gomez)
- www.jonathonhemingray.co.uk (wood sculpture)
- www.bbc.co.uk/learningzone/clips/the-acts-of-the-apostles/4153.html (letters of the New Testament)
- www.e-n.org.uk/p-5-Lord-for-the-years.htm (inspiration for Timothy Dudley-Smith's hymn)
- www.walktherainbow.info/en/theway2go/content/main_JU.html ('The Hub' justice pages)
- http://request.org.uk (search for William Wilberforce, Thomas Barnardo, Elizabeth Fry, George Muller, William Booth) (famous Christians)
- www.walktherainbow.info/en/theway2go/content/main_KG.html ('The Hub': click on 'Creed')
- www.bbc.co.uk/learningzone/clips/the-rough-guide-to-prayer/2871.html (explanation of prayer)
- www.bridge-house.org.uk/ethos/celtic-christian-spirituality (Celtic Christianity)
- http://en.wikipedia.org/wiki/Timeline_of_Christian_missions (information on the spread of Christianity)
- http://web.cocc.edu/cagatucci/classes/hum213/Maps/Maps2HistoryAncient.htm (scroll down to find a map of the spread of early Christianity)
- www.aidanandhilda.org/public_html/web/about-main.php (scroll down for a Celtic timeline PowerPoint file)
- http://request.org.uk/issues/2013/12/06/reflections (questions for Christian visitors)
- http://request.org.uk/oldsite/unpacked/teachings/difference/difference.htm (questions for Christian visitors)
- http://request.org.uk/oldsite/main/dowhat/volunteers/volunteer00.htm (questions for Christian visitors)
- http://request.org.uk/life/pilgrimage-life/2013/07/11/pilgrimage (pilgrimage film clip)
- http://request.org.uk/teachers/wp-content/uploads/sites/2/2013/10/Pilgrimage---lesson-plan.pdf (or search for 'pilgrimage images' in the 'Teachers' area) (pilgrimage lesson plan, images and activity)
- http://request.org.uk/teachers/wp-content/uploads/sites/2/2013/10/thinkthrough_pilgrimage.pdf (pilgrimage statements for diamond-sorting)
- www.taize.fr/en (music from Taizé)
- www.taize.fr/en_article15200.html ('Life in Taizé: stories and personal accounts')
- www.taize.fr/en_rubrique9.html (information for young pilgrims about visits to Taizé)
- www.larche.org.uk (L'Arche communities)
- www.jean-vanier.org/en/home (L'Arche communities)
- www.larche.org.uk/video.php (videos about volunteering and the community)
- www.churchofengland.org/prayer-worship/worship/texts/daily2/morneve.aspx (*Common Worship* Evening Prayer)
- www.michiganstainedglass.org/month/month.php?month=06&year=2010 (Pilgrim's Progress window)

NB: All web links are correct at time of going to press.